GEORGE WASHINGTON'S RULES OF CIVILITY

TRACED TO THEIR SOURCES AND RESTORED

By MONCURE D. CONWAY

INSCRIBED

TO MY SON

EUSTACE CONWAY

George Washington's Rules of Civility
By Moncure D. Conway

Print ISBN 13: 978-1-4209-6315-1
eBook ISBN 13: 978-1-4209-6316-8

This edition copyright © 2019. Digireads.com Publishing.

Cover Image: a detail of "George Washington visiting Bartram's Garden in 1787", painted 1900 (oil on canvas), by Jean Leon Gerome Ferris (1863-1930) / National Museum of American Art, Smithsonian Institute, USA / Bridgeman Images.

Please visit *www.digireads.com*

THE RULES OF CIVILITY.

Among the manuscript books of George Washington, preserved in the State Archives at Washington City, the earliest bears the date, written in it by himself, 1745. Washington was born February 11, 1731 O.S., so that while writing in this book he was either near the close of his fourteenth, or in his fifteenth, year. It is entitled "Forms of Writing," has thirty folio pages, and the contents, all in his boyish handwriting, are sufficiently curious. Amid copied forms of exchange, bonds, receipts, sales, and similar exercises, occasionally, in ornate penmanship, there are poetic selections, among them lines of a religious tone on "True Happiness." But the great interest of the book centres in the pages headed: "Rules of Civility and Decent Behaviour in Company and Conversation." The book had been gnawed at the bottom by Mount Vernon mice, before it reached the State Archives, and nine of the 110 Rules have thus suffered, the sense of several being lost.

The Rules possess so much historic interest that it seems surprising that none of Washington's biographers or editors should have given them to the world. Washington Irving, in his "Life of Washington," excites interest in them by a tribute, but does not quote even one. Sparks quotes 57, but inexactly, and with his usual literary manipulation; these were reprinted (1886, 16°) by W.O. Stoddard, at Denver, Colorado; and in Hale's "Washington" (1888). I suspect that the old biographers, more eulogistic than critical, feared it would be an ill service to Washington's fame to print all of the Rules. There might be a scandal in the discovery that the military and political deity of America had, even in boyhood, written so gravely of the hat-in-hand deference due to lords, and other "Persons of Quality," or had concerned himself with things so trivial as the proper use of the fork, napkin, and toothpick. Something is said too about "inferiours," before whom one must not "Act ag$^{tt.}$ y$^{e.}$ Rules Moral." But in 1888 the Rules were subjected to careful and literal treatment by Dr. J.M. Toner, of Washington City, in the course of his magnanimous task of preserving, in the Library of Congress, by exact copies, the early and perishing note-books and journals of Washington. This able literary antiquarian has printed his transcript of the Rules (W.H. Morrison: Washington, D.C. 1888), and the pamphlet, though little known to the general public, is much valued by students of American history. With the exception of one word, to which he called my attention, Dr. Toner has given as exact a reproduction of the Rules, in their present damaged condition, as can be made in print. The illegible parts are precisely indicated, without any conjectural insertions, and young Washington's spelling and punctuation subjected to no literary tampering.

Concerning the source of these remarkable Rules there have been several guesses. Washington Irving suggests that it was probably his intercourse with the Fairfax family, and his ambition to acquit himself well in their society, that set him upon "compiling a code of morals and manners." (Knickerbocker Ed. i. p. 30.) Sparks, more cautiously, says: "The most remarkable part of the book is that in which is compiled a system of maxims and regulations of conduct, drawn from miscellaneous sources." (i. p. 7.) Dr. Toner says: "Having searched in vain to find these rules in print, I feel justified, considering all the circumstances, in assuming that they were compiled by George Washington himself when a schoolboy. But while making this claim it is proper to state, that nearly all the principles incorporated and injunctions, given in these 110 maxims had been enunciated over and over again in the various works on good behaviour and manners prior to this compilation and for centuries observed in polite society. It will be noticed that, while the spirit of these maxims is drawn chiefly from the social, life of Europe, yet, as formulated here, they are as broad as civilization itself, though a few of them are especially applicable to Society as it then existed in America, and, also, that but few refer to women."

Except for the word "parents," which occurs twice, Dr. Toner might have said that the Rules contain no allusion whatever to the female sex. This alone proved, to my own mind, that Washington was in nowise responsible for these Rules. In the school he was attending when they were written there were girls; and, as he was rather precocious in his admirations, a compilation of his own could hardly omit all consideration of conduct towards ladies, or in their presence. There were other reasons also which led me to dissent from my friend Dr. Toner, in this instance, and to institute a search, which has proved successful, for the source of the Rules of Civility.

While gathering materials for a personal and domestic biography of Washington,[1] I discovered that in 1745 he was attending school in Fredericksburg, Virginia. The first church (St. George's) of the infant town was just then finished, and the clergyman was the Rev. James Marye, a native of France. It is also stated in the municipal records of the town that its first school was taught by French people, and it is tolerably certain that Mr. Marye founded the school soon after his settlement there as Rector, which was in 1735, eight years after the foundation of Fredericksburg. I was thus led to suspect a French origin of the Rules of Civility. This conjecture I mentioned to my friend Dr. Garnett, of the British Museum, and, on his suggestion, explored an old work in French and Latin in which ninety-two of the Rules were found.

---

[1] George Washington and Mount Vernon. A collection of Washington's unpublished agricultural and personal letters. Edited, with historical and genealogical Introduction, by Moncure Daniel Conway. Published by the L.I. Historical Society: Brooklyn, New York, 1889.

This interesting discovery, and others to which it led, enable me to restore the damaged manuscript to completeness.

The various intrinsic interest of these Rules is much enhanced by the curious story of their migration from an old Jesuit College in France to the copy-book of George Washington. In Backer's Jesuit Bibliography it is related that the "pensionnaires" of the College of La Flèche sent to those of the College at Pont-à-Mousson, in 1595, a treatise entitled: "Bienseance de la Conversation entre les Hommes." The great Mussipontane father at that time was Léonard Périn (b. at Stenai 1567, d. at Besançon 1658), who had been a Professor of the Humanities at Paris. By order of Nicolas François, Bishop of Toul, Father Périn translated the La Flèche treatise into Latin, adding a chapter of his own on behaviour at table. The book, dedicated to the Bishop of Toul, was first printed (16°) at Pont-à-Mousson in 1617, (by Car. Marchand). It was printed at Paris in 1638, and at Rouen in 1631; it was translated into Spanish, German, and Bohemian. In 1629 one Nitzmann printed the Latin, German, and Bohemian translations in parallel columns, the German title being "Wolstand taglicher Gemainschafft mit dem Menschen." A comparison of this with the French edition of 1663 in the British Museum, on which I have had to depend, shows that there had been no alteration in Father Périn's Latin, though it is newly translated. This copy in the library of the British Museum was printed in Paris for the College of Clermont, and issued by Pierre de Bresche, "auec privilege du Roy." It is entitled: "Les Maximes de la Gentillesse et de l'Honnesteté en la Conversation entre les Hommes. Communis Vitæ inter homines scita urbanitas. Par un Père de la Compagnie de Jesus."

In dedicating this new translation (1663) to the youth of Clermont, Pierre de Bresche is severe on the French of the La Flèche pensionnaires. "It is a novelty surprising enough to find a very unpolished French book translated into the most elegant Latin ever met with." M. de Bresche declares that he was no longer able to leave so beautiful a work in such "abjection," and had added a translation which preserves the purity of the French tongue, and is proportioned to the merit of the exquisite Latin expressions. We can hardly suppose that Pierre de Bresche was eulogising his own work, but there is no other name in the book. Possibly his criticism on the French of the original edition was only that of an *editeur* desiring to supplant it. At any rate, as Father Périn wrote the elegant Latin we cannot doubt that the chapter he added to the book was in scholarly French.

The old book of the Jesuit "pensionnaires,"—which, had they not ignored woman, might be called the mother of all works on Civility,— is charming as well as curious. It duly opens with a chapter of religious proprieties, at mass, sacrament, sermon, and grace at meat. The Maxims of secular civility open with the second chapter, and it will be seen that they are for the gentry. They are mainly for youths whose environments are portrayed in the interesting frontispiece of the work, where they are seen in compartments,—at church, in college, in conversation, at the fireside, in promenade, and at table. We have already seen, from Backer's Jesuit bibliography, that Father Léonard Périn added a chapter on "bienséance" at table; but after this there is another chapter—a wonderful chapter—and it would be interesting to learn whether we owe this also to Périn. This last chapter is exquisitely epicurean, dealing with table-setting, table-service, and the proper order of entrees, roasts, salads, and dessert. It closes—and the book closes—with a sort of sugarplum paean, the sweets and spices being in the end gracefully spiritualised. But this concluding passage of Chapter XI. ("Des Services & honneurs de la Table") must be quoted:—

"Sugar-plums complete the pleasantness and enjoyment of the dessert, and serve, as it were, to satisfy pleasure. They are brought, while the table is still laid, in a handsome box on a salver, like those given by the ancients to be carried home.[2] Sometimes, also, they are handed round after the hands have been washed in rose water, and the table covered with a Turkey cloth.

"These are riches which we possess in abundance, and your feasts cannot terminate more agreeably in your quarters than with our Verdun sugar-plums. Besides the exquisite delicacy of their sugar, cinnamon and aniseed, they possess a sweet, fragrant odour like the breeze of the Canaries,—that is to say, like our sincerest attachment for you, of which you will also receive proof. Thus you see, then, the courteous advice we have undertaken to give you to serve for a profitable entertainment, If you please, then, we will bring it to a close, in order to devote ourselves more zealously to other duties which will contribute to your satisfaction, and prove agreeable to all those who truly esteem good-breeding and decent general conversation, as we ardently hope.

"Praise be to God and to the glorious Virgin!"[3]

---

[2] This is not unknown at some of the civic banquets in London.

[3] "Les dragées acheuent la douceur de la resjoüissance du dessert & font comme l'assouuissement du plaisir. Elles sont portées dans vne belle boêtte posées sur vn plat, les tables restans encore dressées à la façon de celles que les Anciens donnoient à emporter en la maison. Quelquefois aussi les mains estants desia lauées auec l'eau-rose, & la table couuerte de son tapis de Turquie, elle sont presentées.

"Ce sont des richesses que nous possedons en abondance & vos festins ne se peuuent pas terminer plus agreablement que par nos dragées de Verdun en vos quartiers. Elles sont parmy les charmantes delicatesses de leur succre, de leur canelle, & de leur anis, vne douce & suaue odeur qui égale celles de l'air de nos Canaries, c'est à dire de nos plus sinceres inclinations en vostre endroit dont vous receuerez de mesme les tesmoignages. Vous voyez donc icy les advis de la ciuilité que nous auons entrepris de vous donner, pour vous servir d'vn fructueux divertissement. Nous les finissons donc si vous le trouuiez agreable, pour nous porter auec plus de zele aux autres deuoirs qui contribuëront

The earlier editions of the book do not appear to have been published for the outer world, but were printed in the various colleges where they were used. Another French work on the same subject, but including much about ladies, published about the year 1773, plagiarises largely from the Jesuit manual, but does not mention it. It is probable therefore that the Périn volume was not then known to the general public. The anonymous book just mentioned was translated into English.[4] Some of the phraseology of the Perin book, and many of its ideas, appear in a work of Obadiah Walker, Master of University College, Oxford, on Education, but it is not mentioned.[5] Eighteen of the Washington Rules, and an important addition to another, are not among the French Maxims. Two of these Rules, 24 and 42, are more damaged than any others in the Washington MS., and I had despaired of discovering their meaning. But after my translations were in press I learned from Dr. W.C. Minor that an early English version of the Maxims existed, and in this I have found additions to the French, work which substantially include those of the Washington MS. Through this fortunate discovery the Rules of Civility are now completely restored.

The version just alluded to purports to be by a child in his eighth year. It was first printed in 1640 (London), but the earliest edition in the British Museum, where alone I have been able to find a copy, is that of 1646, which is described as the fourth edition.[6] The cover is stamped in

---

à vostre satisfaction, & qui seront agreables à touts les veritables estimateurs de la bien-seance & de l'honnesteté de la conuersation commune, comme nous le soutraitions auec passion.

"Loüange à Dieu & à la glorieuse Vierge."

[4] "The Rules of Civility, or Certain Ways of Deportment observed amongst all persons of Quality upon seueral Occasions." The earliest edition I have found is that of 1678 (in the British Museum Library), which is said to be "Newly revised and much Enlarged." The work is assigned a French origin on internal evidence,—*e.g.*, other nations than France are referred to as "foreign," and "Monsieur" is used in examples of conversation. The date is approximately fixed as 1673, because it is said that while it was in press there had appeared "The Education of a Young Prince." The latter work was a translation of "De l'education d'un Prince. Par le Sieur de Chanteresne" [P. Nicole], by Pierre du Moulin, the Younger, and published in London, 1673.

[5] Of Education. Especially of Young Gentlemen. In two Parts. The Fifth Impression. Oxford: Published at the Theatre for Amos Custeyne. 1887. [It was anonymous, but is known to be by Obadiah Walker, Master of University College, Oxford.]

[6] "Youth's Behaviour, or Decency in Conversation amongst men. Composed in French by grave persons for the Use and benefit of their youth. Now newly translated into English by Francis Hawkins. The fourth edition, with the addition of twenty-six new Precepts (which are marked thus *) London. Printed by W. Wilson for W. Lee, and are to be sold at the *Turks-head* neere the *Miter Taverne* in *Fleetstreet*. 1646." There are some lines "In laudem Authoris" by J.S., and the following:—"Gentle Reader,—Thinke it not amisse to peruse this Peece, yet connive at the Style: for it hath neede thereof, since wrought by an uncouth and rough File of one greene in yeares; as being aged under eight.

gilt, "Gift of G. III." The translations are indeed rude, and sometimes inaccurate as to the sense, but that they were the unaided work of a child under eight is one of the "things hard to be believed" which a Maxim admonishes us not to tell. In the edition of 1651 there is a portrait of Master Hawkins at the age of eight, and the same picture appears in 1672 as the same person at ten. Moreover, in an edition of 1663 the "Bookseller," in an address "to the reader," seems rather vague in several statements. "A counsellor of the Middle Temple, in 1652, added twenty-five new Precepts marked thus (*) at which time a Gentleman of *Lincoln's*-Inn turned the Book into Latine." There are, however, in this edition thirty-one Precepts not in the French work, and of these twenty-six are in the edition of 1646. The Latin version appended (signed H.B.) is exactly that of Father Périn, with the exception of a few words, considerable omissions, and the additional Precepts. The additions are all evidently by a mature hand.

With the Hawkins volume of 1663 is bound, in the British Museum Library, a companion work, entitled, "The second Part of Youth's Behaviour, or Decency in Conversation amongst Women. 1664." This little book is apparently by Robert Codrington, whose name is signed to its remarkable dedicatory letter: "To the Mirrour of her Sex Mrs. Ellinor Pargiter, and the most accomplished with all reall Perfections Mrs. Elizabeth Washington, her only Daughter, and Heiress to the truly Honourable Laurence Washington Esquire, lately deceased."

This was Laurence Washington of Garsden, Wilts., who married Elianor. second daughter of Wm. Gyse; their only child, a daughter, having married Robert Shirley, Earl Ferrars. Laurence Washington died Jan. 17, 1662, and his widow married Sir William Pargiter.[7]

In a letter to the New York *Nation* (5th June 1890), I said: "Though my theory, that the Rev. James Marye taught Washington these 'Rules,' has done good service in leading to the discovery of their origin, it cannot be verified, unless the clergyman's descendants have preserved papers in which they can be traced." I have since learned from the family that no such papers exist. The discovery just mentioned, that a Part Second of Youth's Behaviour was published in 1664, and dedicated to two ladies of the Washington family in England, lends force to Dr. Minor's suggestion that Washington might have worked out his Rules from the Hawkins version. It would be natural

---

Hence, worthy Reader, shew not thy self too-too-rigid a Censurer. This his version is little dignified, and therefore likely will it appears to thee much imperfect. It ought to be his own, or why under the Title is his name written? Peradventure thou wilt say, what is it to me? yet heare: Such is it really, as that I presume the Author may therein be rendred faithfully: with this courteously be then satisfied.—This small Treatise in its use, will evidently appear to redound to the singular benefit of many a young spirit, to whom solely and purposely it is addressed. Passe it therefore without mistake and candidly."

[7] See "An Examination of the English Ancestry of George Washington. By Henry F. Waters, A.M., Boston. New England Historic Genealogical Society, 1889."

that Part II. so dedicated should be preserved in the Virginia family, and should be bound up with Part I., published the year before, as it is bound in the British Museum. It is certain that one of the later editions of the Hawkins version was used in the preparation of Washington's "Rules," for the eighteen Rules not in the French book are all from "Youth's Behaviour" (1663). Moreover, the phraseology is sometimes the same, and one or two errors of translation follow the Hawkins version. *E.g.*, Maxim ii. 16 begins: "Prenez garde de vous échauffer trop au jeu, & aux emportements qui s'y eleuet." The second clause, a warning against being too much carried away by excitements of play, is rendered by Hawkins, "Contend not, nor speake louder than thou maist with moderation;" and in the Washington MS., "affect not to Speak Louder than ordenary."

A careful comparison, however, of Washington's Rules with the Hawkins version renders it doubtful whether the Virginia boy used the work of the London boy. The differences are more than the resemblances. If in some cases the faults of the Washington version appear gratuitous, the printed copy being before him, on the other hand it often suggests a closer approach to the French—of which language Washington is known to have been totally ignorant. As to the faults, where Hawkins says ceremonies "are too troublesome," Washington says they "is troublesome;" where the former translates correctly that one must not approach where "another readeth a letter," Washington has "is writing a letter;" where he writes "infirmityes" Washington has "Infirmaties;" the printed "manful" becomes "manfull," and "courtesy" "curtesie." Among the variations which suggest a more intimate knowledge of French idioms than that of Hawkins the following may be mentioned. The first Maxim with which both versions open is: "Que toutes actions qui se font publiquement fassent voir son sentiment respectueux à toute la compagnie." Hawkins: "Every action done in view of the world ought to be accompanied with some signe of reverence which one beareth to all who are present." Washington: "Every action done in company ought to be with some sign of respect to those that are present." Here the restoration of "respectueux," and the limitation of "publiquement" by "compagnie," make the latter rendering much neater. In Maxim viii. 47, which admonishes one not to be angry at table, it is said, "bien si vous vous fâchez," you are not to show it. Hawkins translates "if so bee thou bee vexed;" but Washington more finely, "if you have reason to be so, Shew it not." Or compare the following versions of "Si vous vous reposez chez vous, ayât quelque siege, faites en sorte de traiter chacun selõ son merite." Hawkins: "if there be anything for one to sit on, be it a chair, be it a stool, give to each one his due." Washington: "when you present seats let it be to every one according to his degree." Rule 45, for "moderation et douceur" has "Sweetness and Mildness," Hawkins only "sweetness."

Again: "si vous rencontrez ioliment, si vous donnez quelque bon-mot, en faisant rire les autres, empeschez-vous-en, le plus qu'il vous sera possible." Hawkins: "When so it falleth out that thou deliver some happy lively an jolly conceit abstaine thou, and let others laugh." Washington: "if you Deliver anything witty and Pleasent abtain from laughing thereat yourself."

Yet how curt is the version last quoted, and how blundering the sentence! Washington's spelling was always faulty, but it is not characteristic of him to write "abtain" for "abstain." This is one of many signs of haste, suggesting that his pen was following oral instruction. The absence of punctuation is normal; in some cases words have dropped out: such clerical mistakes occur as "eys," "but" for "put," "top" for "of," "whth" for "without," and "affection" for "affectation"—the needed letters being in the last case interlined. Except as regards punctuation, no similar errors occur in any manuscript from Washington's hand, either in youth or age. Another reason for supposing that he may have been following an instructor is the excessive abbreviation. It was by no means characteristic of Washington to suppress details, but here his condensation sometimes deprives maxims of something of their force, if not of their sense. *E.g.,* Rule 59: "Never express anything unbecoming, nor Act ag$^{tt.}$ y^e Rules Moral before your inferiours." *Cf.* Hawkins: "Never expresse anything unbeseeming, nor act against the Rules morall, before thy inferiours, for in these things, thy own guilt will multiply Crimes by example, and as it were, confirme Ill by authority." And "Shift not yourself in the sight of others" hardly does duty for the precept, "It is insufferable impoliteness to stretch the body, extend the arms, and assume different postures." There are, however, but few instances in which the sense of the original has been lost; indeed, the rendering of the Washington MS. is generally an improvement on the original, which is too diffuse, and even more an improvement on the Hawkins version.

Indeed, although Washington was precocious,—a surveyor at seventeen,—it would argue qualities not hitherto ascribed to him were we to suppose that, along with his faulty grammar and spelling, he was competent at fourteen for such artistic selection and prudent omission as are shown by a comparison of his 110 Rules with the 170 much longer ones of the English version. The omission of religious passages, save the very general ones with which the Rules close, and of all scriptural ones, is equally curious whether we refer the Rules to young Washington or to the Rector who taught him. But it would be of some significance if we suppose the boy to have omitted the precept to live "peeceably in that vocation unto which providence hath called thee;" and still more that he should have derived nothing from the following: "Do not think thou canst be a friend to the King whilst thou art an enemy to God: if thy crying iniquity should invite God's judgments to the Court, it would cost thy Soveraigne dear, to give them entertainment." If Washington was acquainted with Part II. of "Youth's Behaviour," relating to women and dedicated to ladies of the Washington race, it is remarkable that no word relating to that sex is found among his Rules.[8]

On the whole, though it is very uncertain, the balance of probabilities seems to favour the theory that the Rules of Civility, found in a copy-book among school exercises, exceedingly abbreviated, and marked by clerical errors unusual with Washington, were derived from the oral teachings of his preceptor; that this Frenchman utilised (and was once or twice misled by) the English version along with the original, which had been used as a manual in his Rouen College.

The Marie family of Rouen,—from which came the Maryes of Virginia,—is distinguished both in Catholic and Huguenot annals. Among the eminent Jesuit authors was Pierre Marie, who was born at Rouen, 1589, and died at Bourges, 1645. He was author of "La Sainte Solitude; ou les Entretiens solitaires de l'ame," and of "La Science du Crucifix: en forme de méditations." The family was divided by the Huguenot movement, and a Protestant branch took root in England. Concerning the latter, Agnew (*French Protestant Exiles*, i. p. 100) gives the following information:—

"Jean Marie, pasteur of Lion-sur-mer, was a refugee in England from the St. Bartholomew massacre. He is supposed to have belonged to the same family as the Huguenot martyr, Marin Marie, a native of St. George in the diocese of Lisieux. It was in the year 1559 that that valiant man, who had become a settler in Geneva, was arrested at Sens when on a missionary journey to France, laden with a bale of Bibles and New Testaments, and publications for the promotion of the Protestant Reformation; he was burnt at Paris, in the place Maubert, on the 3d of August of that year. Our pasteur was well received in England, and was sent to Norwich, of which city he appears to have been the first French minister. He was lent to the reformed churches of France when liberty of preaching revived, and so returned to Normandy, where we find him in 1583. The first National Synod of

---

[8] In the edition of Hawkins (1663) bound up with Part II. in the British Museum (bearing on the cover the name and arms of the "Hon'ble Thos. Greville") there is just one precept concerning women: "If thou art yet unmarried, but intendest to get thee a wife modest, rather than beautiful, meddle not with those Ladies of the Game, who make pageants of their Cheeks, and Shops of their Shoulders, and (contrary to all other Trades) keep open their Windows on the Sabbath-day, impudently exposing their nakedness to the view of a whole Congregation," &c. There are, in an appendix, pictures of a puritanically shrouded "Virtue," and a "Vice" who, apart from the patches on her face, singularly resembles a portrait of pretty Lady Ferrars in Codrington's book (*ante*, p. 21) ed. 1672.

Vitré held its meetings in that year, between the 15th and 27th of May. Quick's 'Synodicon' (vol. i. p. 153) quotes the following minute:— 'Our brother, Monsieur Marie, minister of the church of Norwich in England, but living at present in Normandy, shall be obliged to return unto his church upon its first summons; yet, because of the great success of his ministry in these parts, his church may be entreated to continue for some longer time his absence from it.' He certainly did return to Norwich, because on 29th April 1589 the manuscript Book of Discipline was submitted to the consistory for signature; and Jan Marie signed first, and his colleague M. Basnage, second. One of his sons, Nathaniel Marie, became one of the pasteurs of the London French Church, and married 1st, Ester, daughter of the pasteur Guillaume De Laune, and 2dly (in 1637), Ester le Hure, widow of André Joye. The Norwich pasteur had probably another son named after himself, a commercial residenter in his native city; for two sons of a Jan Marie were baptized in Norwich French Church: (1) Jan on 3d February 1600, and (2) Pierre, on 6th July 1602. Madame Marie, probably the pasteur's widow, was a witness at the first baptism."

James Marye, with whom we are particularly concerned, sprang from the Catholic family, and was born at Rouen near the close of the seventeenth century. He was educated for the priesthood, no doubt at the Jesuit College in Rouen,—where, as we have seen, Father Périn's book on manners was printed in 1651. However, James Marye abjured the Catholic religion in 1726. This caused a breach between himself and the family, which consisted of a widowed mother and her two other sons,—Peter and William (the latter an officer), both of whose names however, reappeared in their protestant brother's family. In consequence of this alienation James migrated to England, where he pursued his studies, and was ordained by the Bishop of London. In 1728 he married Letitia Maria Anne Staige. She was a sister of the Rev. Theodosius Staige, who was already in Virginia. For that colony the Rev. James Marye also embarked, in 1729, with his bride. Their first child (Lucy) was born during the voyage.

It would appear that the purpose of this emigration was to minister to a settlement of French Huguenots at Monacan (or Manakintown, as it was called) on James River. The first band of these refugees had gone over in 1690, under the leadership of Olivier de la Muce, and 600 others had followed in 1699, with their clergyman, Phillipe de Richebourg. The Assembly of Virginia gave them a large tract of land in Henrico County—not far from where Richmond now stands— exempting them from taxation. The name of James Marye first appears in Virginia (1730) as christening a child in King William Parish, as it was called,—after the King who had favoured this Huguenot colony.

In 1727 the town of Fredericksburg was founded. In 1732 Col.

Byrd visited the place, and wrote: "Besides Col. Willis, who is the top man of the place, there are only one merchant, a tailor, a smith, an ordinary keeper, and a lady who acts both as a doctress and coffeewoman." This "Col. Willis" had married Washington's aunt (and godmother), and there were other families of the neighbourhood connected with the Washingtons. It was not until 1739 that Captain Augustine Washington (the General's father) went to reside near Fredericksburg. Soon after the birth of George (Feb. 11, 1731 Old Style) the family left their homestead in Westmoreland county, Virginia, and resided on their farm, now known as "Mount Vernon." (It was so named by Washington's elder half-brother, Lawrence, who built the mansion, in 1743-5, in honour of the English Admiral Vernon, with whom he served as an officer at Carthagena.) Although he nowhere alludes to the fact, George Washington's earliest memories, as I have elsewhere shown,[9] were associated with the estate on which he lavished so much devotion, and which the Ladies' Mount Vernon Association has made his most characteristic monument. The Rev. Jonathan Boucher, teacher of Mrs. George Washington's son John Custis, says that Washington was "taught by a convict servant whom his father had bought for a schoolmaster." This was probably one of a shipload of convicts brought by Captain Augustine Washington from England in 1737. When the family removed to the neighbourhood of Fredericksburg (from which, however, they were separated by the Rappahannock river), the children went to school (probably) at Falmouth,—a village fifty years older than Fredericksburg, and about two miles above, on the opposite side of the river. A church had been erected in Falmouth (Brunswick parish), but that in Fredericksburg was not completed until some years later. After the death of his father (April 12, 1743) George was sent to reside with his half-brother Augustine, at "Wakefield," the old homestead in Westmoreland where he was born. He returned to live with his mother near Fredericksburg, in 1715. That he then went to school in Fredericksburg appears by a manuscript left by Col. Byrd Willis, grandson of Col. Harry Willis, founder of the town, in which he states that his father, Lewis Willis was Washington's schoolmate. The teachers name is not given, but there can be little doubt that it was James Marye.

The Rev. James Marye's brother-in-law, Rev. Theodosius Staige, had for a time preached in the temporary structure in which the congregation of St. George's, Fredericksburg, met before the church was completed. It was probably during a visit to Mr. Staige that Mr. Marye made an impression on the people of that place. At any rate the early Vestry-book shows that, in 1735, the churchwardens, after the colonial custom, asked leave of the Governor of Virginia to call James

---

[9] George Washington and Mount Vernon. Introduction, p. xxvii.

Marye to their pulpit, and it was granted. He is described as "Mr. Marie of St. James," being then officiating at St James Church, Northam Parish (Goochland county, Virginia). At what time and why he left Manakintown is not clear. He fixed his first abode eight miles out of Fredericksburg, in a place which he called "Fayetteville;" and it is not improbable that some of his Huguenot congregation had come with him, and attempted to found there a village. Several infant churches in the county (Spottsylvania), besides that of Fredericksburg, were under supervision of the Rector of St. George's Parish.

The Rev. James Marye remained in active and successful ministry at Fredericksburg from 1735 until his death, in 1767. He founded the large Virginia family which bears his name, and which has always had eminent representatives. On his death he was succeeded in St. George's Church, Fredericksburg, by his son of the same name, whose honourable tradition was maintained. His great-grandson, John L. Marye,—whose mansion, "Brompton," stood on "Marye's Heights," so famous in the Civil War,—was an eminent lawyer; as also is a son of the latter, John L. Marye Jr., former Lieutenant-Governor of Virginia.[10]

The founder of the Virginia Maryes, who should be ranked among American worthies, was an eloquent clergyman, and built up a noble congregation in Fredericksburg. He was also an accomplished gentleman and a scholar. That he founded and taught the school is tolerably certain. The Municipal Records, as we have seen, ascribe the school a French origin. The name and condition of every respectable resident of Fredericksburg, at the time of his settling there, when it was little more than a "paper town" (in colonial phrase), is known. There was in the place no one—certainly no "Frenchman"—except Marye who could have taught a school of such importance as that at Fredericksburg. For it presently became known throughout Virginia as the chief Academy, especially for classical education, and its reputation continued for more than a hundred years.[11]

Some of the Rules may strike the modern reader as snobbish, even for the observance of youth. But the originals are in that respect toned down in Washington's MS. Rule 9 takes no cognizance of the principle of the original, that to approach nearer the fire than others, and to turn one's back to it are privileges of persons of rank. The 17th Maxim of chapter iii., which directed certain kissings of the hands of superiors, or

---

[10] For valuable information concerning the Marye family and its descendants, see Brock's "Huguenot Emigration to Virginia." (Virginia Hist. Soc., Richmond, 1886.)

[11] In a note I have from John L. Marye (sometime Lieutenant-Governor of Virginia), he says: "As to the habit of the Parish Minister to conduct or overlook the schools, it would appear must probable that this was the case in 1745, when we remember how destitute at that era colonial society was of well-organized public or private schools (save the Tutors in families). When I entered Mr. Hanson's school in 1834, it was the custom of Parson McGuire and some of the Vestry to attend the annual Examinations."

of the robe, and other abasements, is entirely omitted. Where the original commands that we should never dispute in any fashion with our superiors in rank, Rule 34 says we ought not to "begin" with them. The only thing clear about which is that the instructor did not wish to admit authority so absolutely into the realm of argument. Rule 46 omits so much of the original as counsels grateful acceptance of reproof from another "the more if you depend on his authority." Other instances of this more liberal tendency will be noticed by those who make a careful comparison of the Rules and the French Maxims.

Here then are rules of conduct, taught, if my theory be correct, by a French protestant pilgrim, unknown to fame, in the New World. They were taught to a small school of girls and boys, in a town of hardly a hundred inhabitants. They are maxims partly ethical, but mainly relate to manners and civility; they are wise, gentle, and true. A character built on them would be virtuous, and probably great. The publisher of the English version (1665) says that "Mr. Pinchester, a learned scholar of Oxford," bought 250 copies for a great school he was about to open in London. Probably the school founded by James Marye was the first in the New World in which good manners were seriously taught.[12] Nay, where is there any such school to day?

Just this one colonial school, by the good fortune of having for its master or superintendent an ex-jesuit French scholar, we may suppose instructed in civility; and out of that school, in what was little more than a village, came an exceptionally large number of eminent men. In that school three American Presidents received their early education,— Washington, Madison, and Monroe.

It may be pretty confidently stated that both Madison and Monroe owed their success and eminence more to their engaging manners than to great intellectual powers. They were even notably deficient in that oratorical ability which counted for so much in the political era with which they were connected. They rarely spoke in Congress. When speaking, Madison was hesitating, and was heard with difficulty; but his quietness and modesty, his consideration for others, made the eloquent speak for him Whether these two statesmen were personally taught by James Marye is doubtful, for he was getting old when they were at school in Fredericksburg; but we may feel sure that civility was

---

[12] It is probable that Mr. Marye's fine precedent was followed, to some extent, in the Fredericksburg Academy. The present writer, who entered it just a hundred years after George Washington recorded the "Rules," recalls, as his first clear remembrance of the school, some words of the worthy Principal, Thomas Hanson, on gentlemanly behaviour. Alluding to some former pupil, who had become distinguished, he said, "I remember, on one occasion, in a room where all were gathered around the fire—the weather being very cold—that some one entered, and this boy promptly arose and gave the new-comer his seat at the fire. It made an impression on me which I have never forgotten." And how long have lasted in the memory of the writer hereof the very words of our teacher's homage to the considerate boy who obeyed Washington's eighth Rule!

still taught there in their time, as, indeed it was within the memory of many now living.

George Washington, though even less able than the two others to speak in public, had naturally a strong intellect. But in boyhood he had much more against him than most of his young comrades,—obstructions that could be surmounted only by character. His father had much land but little money; at his death (1743,) the lands were left chiefly to his sons by the first wife. His widow was left poor, and her eldest son, George, had not the fair prospect of most of his schoolmates. Instead of being prepared for William and Mary College, he was prepared only for going into some business as soon as possible, so as to earn support for his mother and her four younger children. In his old book of school-exercises, the "Rules of Civility" are found in proximity to business forms that bear pathetic testimony to the severe outlook of this boy of fourteen. In the MS. of Col. Byrd Willis, already referred to (loaned me by his granddaughter, Mrs. Tayloe, of Fredericksburg), he says: "My father, Lewis Willis, was a schoolmate of General Washington, his cousin, who was two years his senior. He spoke of the General's industry and assiduity at school as very remarkable. Whilst his brother and other boys at playtime were at bandy and other games, he was behind the door ciphering. But one youthful ebullition is handed down while at that school, and that was romping with one of the largest girls; this was so unusual that it excited no little comment among the other lads." It is also handed down that in boyhood this great soldier, though never a prig, had no fights, and was often summoned to the playground as a peacemaker, his arbitration in disputes being always accepted.

Once more it may be well enough to remind the reader that it may yet be found that Washington, in his mother's humble home on the Rappahannock, read and pondered "Youth's Behaviour," wrote out what it held for him, and himself became an instructor of his schoolmates in rules of civility. It would be wonderful, but not incredible.

Although Washington became a fine-looking man, he was not of prepossessing appearance in early life; he was lank and hollow-chested. He was by no means a favourite with the beauties for which Fredericksburg was always famous, and had a cruel disappointment of his early love for Betsy Fauntleroy. In his youth he became pitted by smallpox while attending his invalid half-brother, Lawrence, on a visit to the Barbadoes.

But the experienced eye of Lord Fairfax, and of other members of the Fairfax family, had discovered beneath the unattractive appearance of George Washington a sterling character. Their neighbourhood, on the upper Potomac, was much less civilised and refined than Fredericksburg, and this young gentleman, so well instructed in right rules of behaviour and conduct, won their hearts and their confidence. It had been necessary that he should leave school at the age of sixteen to earn a living. At seventeen he was appointed by Lord Fairfax surveyor of his vast estates in Virginia, and for a time he resided with his lordship at Greenway Court. There can be little doubt that it was partly through the training in manners which Washington gained from the old French maxims that he thus made headway against circumstances, and gained the friendship of the highly-educated and powerful Fairfax family.

It should be mentioned, however, that young Washington's head was not in the least turned by this intimacy with the aristocracy. He wrote letters to his former playmates in which no snobbish line is discoverable. He writes to his "Dear friend Robin": "My place of residence is at present at his lordship's where I might, was my heart disengaged, pass my time very pleasantly, as there's a very agreeable young lady lives in the same house (Col. George Fairfax's wife's sister). But as that's only adding fuel to fire, it makes me the more uneasy, for by often and unavoidably being in company with her revives my former passion for your Lowland beauty; whereas, was I to live more retired from young women, I might eleviate in some measure my sorrows by burying that chaste and troublesome passion in the grave of oblivion or etearnall forgetfulness, for as I am very well assured, that's the only antidote or remedy that I ever shall be relieved by or only recess that can administer any cure or help to me, as I am well convinced, was I ever to attempt anything, I should only get a denial which would be only adding grief to uneasiness."

The young lady at Greenway Court was Mary Gary, and the Lowland beauty was Betsy Fauntleroy, whose hand Washington twice sought, but who became the wife of the Hon. Thomas Adams. While travelling on his surveys, often among the red men, the youth sometimes gives vent to his feelings in verse.

"Oh Ye Gods why should my Poor resistless Heart
    Stand to oppose thy might and Power
At last surrender to Cupid's feather'd Dart
    And now lays bleeding every Hour
For her that's Pityless of my grief and Woes,
    And will not on me Pity take.
I'll sleep among my most inveterate Foes
    And with gladness never wish to wake,
In deluding sleepings let my Eyelids close
    That in an enraptured dream I may
In a rapt lulling sleep and gentle repose
    Possess those joys denied by Day."

And it must also be recorded that if he had learned how to conduct himself in the presence of persons superior to himself in position, age, and culture,—and it will be remembered that Lord Fairfax was an able contributor to the "Spectator" (which Washington was careful to study while at Greenway,)—this youth no less followed the instruction of his 108th rule: "Honour your natural parents though they be poor." His widowed mother was poor, and she was ignorant, but he was devoted to her; being reverential and gracious to her even when with advancing age she became somewhat morose and exacting, while he was loaded with public cares.

I am no worshipper of Washington. But in the hand of that man of strong brain and powerful passions once lay the destiny of the New World,—in a sense, human destiny. But for his possession of the humility and self-discipline underlying his Rules of Civility, the ambitious politicians of the United States might to-day be popularly held to a much lower standard. The tone of his character was so entirely that of modesty, he was so fundamentally patriotic, that even his faults are transformed to virtues, and the very failures of his declining years are popularly accounted successes. He alone was conscious of his mental decline, and gave this as a reason for not accepting a third nomination for the Presidency. This humility has established an unwritten law of limitation on vaulting presidential ambitions. Indeed, intrigue and corruption in America must ever struggle with the idealised phantom of this grand personality.

These Rules of Civility go forth with the hope that they will do more than amuse the reader by their quaintness, and that their story will produce an impression beyond that of its picturesqueness. The strong probabilities that they largely moulded the character of Washington, and so influenced the human race, may raise the question, whether the old French Jesuits, and the pilgrim, James Marye, did not possess more truly than our contemporary educators, the art and mystery of moral education. In these days, when ethical is replacing theological instruction, in the home and in the school, there appears danger that it may repeat some of the mistakes of its predecessor. The failure of what was called Religion to promote moral culture is now explicable: its scheme of terror and hope appealed to and powerfully stimulated selfishness, and was also fundamentally anti-social, cultivating alienation of all who did not hold certain dogmas. The terrors and hopes having faded away, the selfishness they developed remains, and is only unchained by the decay of superstition. On the other hand, the social sentiment has thrown off sectarian restrictions, and an enthusiasm of humanity has succeeded. It is now certain that the social instinct is the only one which can be depended on to influence conduct to an extent comparable with the sway once exercised by superstitious terrors and expectations of celestial reward. The child is spiritually a creation of the commune; there can be no other motive so early responsive as that which desires the approval and admiration of those by whom it is surrounded.

To attempt the training of human character by means of ethical philosophy or moral science—as it used to be called—appears to be somewhat of a theological "survival." When the sanctions of authority were removed from the pagan deities they were found to have been long reduced in the nursery to the dimensions of fairies. The tremendous conceptions of Christian theology may some day be revealed as similarly diminished in the catechised mind of childhood. And the abstract principles of ethical philosophy cannot hope for any better fate. The child's mind cannot receive the metaphysics of virtue. It is impossible to explain to a child, for instance, the reasons for truthfulness, which, indeed, have grown out of the experience of the human race as matured by many ages. And so of humanity to animals, which is mainly a Darwinian revival of Buddhist sentiment based on a doctrine of transmigration. And the same may be said of other virtues. We must not suppose that a child has no scepticism because he cannot express or explain it in words; it will appear in the sweetness to him of stolen apples, in the fact that to label a thing "naughty" may only render it more tempting to a healthy boy. A philosopher said, "A fence is the temptation to a jump."

Our ethical teaching is vitiated by, an inheritance from theology of a superstition which subordinates conduct to its motives. Really, if conduct be good, the motive (generally too complex for even consciousness to analyse) is of least importance. Motives are important as causing conduct, but the Law is just in assuming good or bad motives for the corresponding actions. The world does not depend on a man's inner but on his outer life. Emerson once scandalised some of his admirers by saying that he preferred a person who did not respect the truth to an unpresentable person. But, no doubt, he would regard the presentable person as possessing virtues of equal importance. The nurture of "civility and decent behaviour in company and conversation," is not of secondary, but primary, importance.

For what does it imply? If the Rules about to be submitted are examined, it will be found that their practice draws on the whole moral world, as in walking every step draws on the universal gravitation. Scarcely one Rule is there that does not involve self-restraint, modesty, habitual consideration of others, and, to a large extent, living for others. Yet other Rules draw on the profounder deeps of wisdom and virtue, under a subtle guise of handsome behaviour. If youth can be won to excellence by love of beauty, who shall gainsay?

It may occur to the polished reader that well-bred youths know and practise these rules of civility by instinct. But the best bred man's ancestors had to learn them, and the rude progenitors of future gentlemen have to learn them. Can it be said, however, that those deemed well-bred do really know and practise these rules of civility instinctively? Do they practise them when out of the region of the persons or the community in whose eyes they wish to find approval? How do they act with Indians, Negroes, or when travelling amongst those to whose good opinion they are indifferent? In a Kentucky court a witness who had spoken of a certain man as "a gentleman," was pressed for his reasons, and answered, "If any man goes to his house he sets out the whisky, then goes and looks out of the window." It is doubtful if what commonly passes for politeness in more refined regions is equally humanised with that of the Kentuckian so described. Indeed the only difficulty in the way of such teaching as is here suggested, is the degree to which the words "lady" and "gentleman" have been lowered from their original dignity.

The utilization of the social sentiment as a motive of conduct in the young need not, however, depend on such terms, though these are by no means beyond new moralization in any home or school. An eminent Englishman told me that he once found his little son pointing an old pistol at his sister. The ancient pistol was not dangerous, but the action was. "Had I told him it was dangerous," he said, "it might only have added spice to the thing, but I said, 'I am surprised. I thought you were a little gentleman, but that is the most ungentlemanly thing you could do.' The boy quickly laid aside the pistol, with deep shame. I have found nothing so restraining for my children as to suggest that any conduct is ungentlemanly or unladylike." And let my reader note well the great moral principles in these rules of civility and decent behaviour. The antithesis of "sinfull" is "manfull." Washington was taught that all good conduct was gentlemanly, all bad conduct ill-bred.

It is to be hoped that the time is not far distant when in every school right rules of civility will be taught as a main part of the curriculum. Something of the kind was done by the late Bronson Alcott, in the school he founded in Boston, Massachusetts, near fifty years ago, for children gathered from the street. The school was opened every morning with a "conduct lesson," as it was called. It will be seen by Miss Elizabeth Peabody's "Records of a School" that the children crowded to the door before it was, opened in their anxiety not to lose a word of this lesson. And, rude as most of the children were, this instruction, consisting of questions and answers, gradually did away with all necessity for corporal punishments.

It were a noble task for any competent hand to adapt the Rules given in this volume, and those of the later French work, and still more those of Master Obadiah Walker's book on "Education," to the conditions and ideas of our time, for the use of schools. From the last-named work, that of a Master of University College, Oxford, I will take for my conclusion a pregnant passage.

"The greatest *Magnetismes* in the World are *Civility*, Conforming to the innocent humours, and infirmities, sometimes, of others, readiness to do courtesies for all, Speaking well of all behind their backs. And sly *Affability*, which is not only to be used in common and unconcerning speech, but upon all occasions. A man may deny a request, chide, reprehend, command &c. *affably*, with good words, nor is there anything so harsh which may not be inoffensively represented."

NOTE.

There has been no alteration of the original French and English documents in the pages following. The spelling, punctuation, use of small or capital letters, italics, etc., whether faults or archaisms, are strictly preserved.

The word 'Maxim' refers to the early French work (of the Jesuit Fathers). 'Rule' refers to Washington's MS.

'Hawkins' indicates the English version of the Maxims, chiefly the anonymous additions thereto. See p. 7.

'Walker' refers to Obadiah Walker's work on Education, spoken of on p. 7.

'The later French book' refers to the anonymous work of 1673, translated into English, mentioned on p. 7.

1st. Every Action done in Company ought to be with Some Sign of Respect, to those that are Present.

MAXIMES, CHAP. II.

Chapter ii. 1. Que toutes actions qui se font publiquement fassent voir son sentiment respectueux à toute la compagnie.

All actions done before others should be with some sign of respectful feeling to the entire company.

2d. When in Company, put not your Hands to any Part of the Body not usually Discovered.

Chapter ii. 3. Gardez-vous bien de toucher de la main aucune partie de vostre corps, de celles qui ne sont point en veuë, en la presence d'aucune autre personne. Pour les mains, & le visage, cela leur est ordinaire. Et afin de vous y accoustumer pratiquez ce poinct de ciuilité mesme en vostre particulier.

In the presence of any one, never put your hand to any part of the person not usually uncovered. As for the hands and face they are usually visible. In order to form a habit in this point of decency, practise it even when with your intimate friend.

3d. Shew Nothing to your Friend that may affright him.

Chapter ii. 4. Ne faites pas voir a vostre compagnon, ce qui luy pourroit faire mal au coeur.

Show nothing to your companion that may grieve him.

4th. In the Presence of Others sing not to yourself with a humming Noise, nor Drum, with your Fingers or Feet.

Chapter ii. 5. Ne vous amusez pas à chanter en vous mesme, si vous ne vous rencontrez si fort à l'écart qu'aucun autre ne vous puisse entendre, non plus qu'à contre-faire le son du tambour par l'agitation des pieds ou des mains.

Do not seek amusement in singing to yourself, unless beyond the hearing of others, nor drum with your hands or feet.

5th. If you Cough, Sneeze, Sigh, or Yawn, do it not Loud, but Privately; and Speak not in your Yawning, but put your handkerchief or Hand before your face and turn aside.

Chapter ii. 8. Quand vous toussez ou quand vous esternuez, si vous pouuez estre le maistre de ces efforts de nature, n'éclatez pas si hautement & si fort. Ne poussez soûpirs si aigres que les autres les puissent entendre.
9. Ne soufflez pas si asprement, faisant des hurlements en baaillant. Et s'il vous est possible, empeschez vous absolum[=e]t de baaailler; mais ayez en un bien plus soin, quand vous entretenez avec quelqu'vn, ou dans quelque conuersation. Car c'est un signe manifest d'un certain dégoust de ceux avec qui vous vivez. Si vous ne pouvez pas empescher de baaailler, du moins gardez vous bien de parler en cet instant mesme, & d'ouurir extraordinairem[=e]t la bouche; mais pressez la sagement, ou en détournant tant soi peu la face de la cõpagnie.

Whenever you cough or sneeze,[13] if you can control these efforts of nature, do not let the sound be high or strong. Do not heave sighs so piercing as to attract attention. Do not breathe heavily, or make noises in yawning. If you can, abstain from yawning, especially while with any one, or in conversation. For it is a plain sign of a certain dislike of those with whom you dwell. If you cannot keep from yawning, at least be careful not to speak while doing so, and not to gape excessively; press your mouth adroitly or n turning a little from the company.

6th. Sleep not when others Speak, Sit not when others stand, Speak not when you should hold your Peace, walk not when others Stop

Chapter ii. 11. C'est vne inciuilité & vne impertinence de dormir, pendant que la cõpagnie s'entretient de discours; de se tenir assis lors que tout le monde est debout, de se promener lors que personne ne branle, & de parler, quãd il est temps de se taire ou d'écouter. Pour celuy toutesfois qui a l'authorité, il y a des temps & des lieux où il luy est permis de se promener seul, comme à un Precepteur qui est dans la classe.

It is an incivility and an impertinence to doze while the company is conversing, to be seated while the rest stand, to walk on when others pause, and to speak when you should be silent, or listen. For those in authority, as a Master in school, there are times and places when it is admissible to walk alone.

7th. Put not off your Cloths in the presence of Others, nor go out of your Chamber half Drest.

Chapter ii. 12. Il n'est pas seant d'auoir son liet en mauuais ordre dans sa chambre, non plus que de s'habiller en la presence des autres, ou de s'y dépoüiller, ou de sortir de sa mesme chambre à demy habillé, couuert de sa coiffe, ou bonnet-de-nuiet, de rester debout en sa chãbre ou estre attaché à son pulpitre auec sa robe ouuerté. Et quoy que vous ne manquiez pas de seruiteur qui prenne le soin de faire vostre liet; toutesfois en sortant, prenez garde de le laisser découuert.

It is not seemly to leave your bed disarranged, to dress or undress before others, or to leave your chamber half-dressed, covered with a hood, or night-cap, or to remain standing in your room or at your desk with open gown. And although you have a servant to make your bed, nevertheless, take care when you go out to leave it uncovered.

---

[13] Sidenote: The later French book advises one, in sneezing, not to shake the foundations of the house.

8th. At Play and at Fire its Good manners to give Place to the last Commer, and affect not to Speak Louder than ordenary.

Chapter ii. 15. Il est mal-seant, dans le jeu, ou aupres du feu de faire attendre trop long-temps ceux qui viennent à s'y presenter.

It is impolite at play, or at the fireside, to make the new-comers wait for places too long.

(In the second clause, "affect not" &c., the Washington MS. follows Hawkins in misunderstanding a phrase of the next Maxim: "Prenez garde de vous échauffer trop au jeu, & aux emportements qui s'y eleuẽt,"—a warning against being overheated at play, and "carried away by its excitements.")

9th. Spit not in the Fire, nor Stoop low before it neither Put your Hands into the Flames to warm them, nor Set your Feet upon the Fire especially if there be meat before it.

Chapter ii. 17. C'est une action peu hõneste de cracher dans la cheminée, d'approcher .ses mains trop prés de la flâme pour les échauffer, & de les mettre même dedans, de se baisser deuãt le feu, comme si l'on estoit assis à terre & s'y tenir courbé. S'il arriue qu'il y ait quelque chose deuant le feu, a cuire, prenez bien garde d'estendre le pied pardessus le feu. Dans une honneste compagnie n'y tournez iamais le dos, & ne vous en approchez point plus prés que les autres : car ce sont des priuileges de personnes qualifiées. Quand il n'en est point besoin, de remuer le feu, y pousser le bois, l'y fourrer plus auant ou l'en leuer, il n'appartient qu'à celuy qui doit auoir le soin de tout ce qui est à faire.

It is not a handsome action to spit in the fireplace, or, in warming the hands, to hold them nearly in the flame, or as if resting on the ground and crouching beside it. If anything is cooked before the fire, do not extend your foot over it. In polite society do not turn your back to the fire, and do not approach it closerthan others; these are privileges of persons of rank. When there is need of stirring the fire, putting wood on it, pulling or lifting it, this belongs to the person who has the general superintendence of those things.[14]

---

[14] Sidenote: The use of the negative in the French original ('n'en est point') seems erroneous, and is disregarded in this translation.

10th. When you Sit down, Keep your Feet firm and Even, without putting one on the other or Crossing them

Chapter ii. 18. Pour l'ordre que l'on doit tenir étant assis, c'est de placer bien ses pieds à terre en égale distance que les cuisses, non pas de croiser vne cuisse ou vn pied sur l'autre.

When seated, the feet should be placed well on the ground, in even distance with the legs, and neither a leg or a foot should be crossed on the other.

11th. Shift not yourself in the Sight of others nor Gnaw your nails.

Chapter ii. 7. C'est vne inciuilité insupportable d'allonger son corps en estendant les bras, ou de faire differents postures.

Chapter iii. 19. Il ne faut iamais rogner ses ongles dans le public, & bien moins les prendre à beiles dents.

It is insufferably impolite to stretch the body, extend the arms, or to assume different postures.

Do not pare your nails in public, much less gnaw them.

12th. Shake not the head, Feet, or Legs rowl not the Eys, lift not one eyebrow higher than the other wry not the mouth, and bedew no mans face with your Spittle, by appr[oaching too nea]r [when] you Speak.

Chapter ii. 21. Vous ne hocherez la teste, vous ne remuerez point les jambes, ny ne roüillerez les yeux, ne froncerez point les sourcils, ou tordrez la bouche. Vous vous garderez de laisser aller auec vos paroles de la saliue, ou du crachat aux visages de ceux, auec qui vous conversez. Pour obvier à cét accident, vous ne vous en approcherez point si prés; mais vous les entretiendrez dans vne distăce raisonnable.

Shake not the head, nor fidget the legs, nor roll the eyes, nor frown, nor make mouths. Be careful not to let saliva escape with your words, nor any spittle fly into the faces of those with whom you converse. To avoid such accident do not approach them too near, but keep at a reasonable distance.

13th. Kill no Vermin as Fleas, lice ticks &c in the Sight of Others, if you See any filth or thick Spittle put your foot Dexteriously upon it if it be upon the Cloths of your Companions, Put it off privately, and if it be upon your own Cloths return Thanks to him who puts it off

Chapter ii. 22. Gardez vous biē de vous arrester à tuër vne puce, ou quelque sale bestiole de cette espece, en presence de qui que a puisse estre. Que si quelque chose d'immõde vient à vous offenser la veuë, en regardant à terre, comme quelque crachat infect, ou quelque autre chose semblable, mettez le pied dessus. S'il en attache quelque'vne aux habits de celuy à qui vous parlez, ou voltige dessus, gardez vouz bien de la luy monstrer, ou à quelqu'autre personne; mais trauaillez autant que vous pourrez à l'oster adroitement. Et s'il arriue que quelqu'vn vous oblige tant que de vous défaire de quelque chose de semblable, faites luy paroistre vostre reconnoissance.

Do not stop to kill a flea, or other disgusting insect of the kind, in the presence of any one. If anything disgusting offends the sight on the ground, as phlegm, etc., put your foot on it. If it be on any garment of one to whom you are talking, do not show it to him or another, but do your best to remove it unobserved. If any one oblige you in a thing of that kind make him your acknowledgments.

14th. Turn not your Back to others especially in Speaking, Jog not the Table or Desk on which Another reads or writes lean not upon any one.

Chapter ii. 24. En la rencontre que l'on fait des personnes, quand on les entretient, c'est une chose malseante de leur tourner le dos & les épaules. C'est vne action impertinente de heurter la table ou d'ébranler le pupitre, dont vn autre se sert pour lire, ou pour écrire. C'est vne inciuilité de s'appuyer sur quelqu'vn, de tirer sa robbe, lors que l'on luy parle ou que l'on le peut entretenir.

When one meets people, it is very unbecoming in speaking to them to turn one's back and shoulders to them. It is an impertinent action to knock against the table, or to shake the desk, which another person is using for reading or writing. It is uncivil to lean against any one, or to pluck his dress when speaking to him, or while entertaining him in conversation.

15th. Keep your Nails clean and Short, also your Hands and Teeth Clean, yet without Shewing any great Concern for them

Chapter ii. 25. Gardez vous bien de vous arrester en toute sorte de conuersation, à rajuster vostre rabat, ou à rehausser vos chausses pour les faire ioindre & en paroitre plus galaud. Que vos ongles ne soient point replis d'ordures, ny trop longs. Ayez grand soin de la netteté de vos mains; mais n'y recherchez point la volupté.

Take good care not to stop, in any sort of conversation, to adjust your bands, or to pull up your stockings to make them join so as to look more gallant. Do not let your nails be full of dirt or too long. Have a great regard for the cleanliness of your hands, but do not be finikin about it.[15]

16th. Do not puff up the Cheeks, Loll not out the tongue rub the Hands, or beard, thrust out the lips, or bite them or keep the lips too open or too close.

Chapter ii. 26. C'est une vilainie de s'enfler les joües, de tirer la langue, de se manier la barbe, se frotter les mains, d'estendre ses levres ou les mordre, de les tenir trop serrées ou trop entrouuertes.

It is very low to puff out the cheeks, to put out the tongue, to pull one's beard, rub one's hands, poke out or bite the lips, or to keep them too tightly closed or too open.

17th. Be no Flatterer, neither Play with any that delights not to be Play'd Withal.

Chapter ii. 27. Ne flattez & n'amadoüez personne par belles paroles, car celui qui pretend d'en gagner un autre par les discours emmiellez, fait voir qu'il n'en a pas grande estime, & qu'il le tient pour peu sensé & adroit, dés qu'il le prend pour vn hõme que l'on peut ioüer en cette maniere: n'usez point de gausseries auprés d'vne personne qui s'en offense.

Do not flatter or wheedle any one with fair words, for he who aspires to gain another person by his honied words shows that he does not hold him in high esteem and that he deems him far from sensible or clever, in taking him for a man who may be tricked in this manner: do not play practical jokes on those who do not like it.

---

[15] Sidenote: Hawkins: "without overmuch attendance thereon or curiosity."

18th. Read no Letters, Books, or Papers in Company but when there is a Necessity for the doing of it you must ask leave: come not near the Books or Writings of Another so as to read them unless desired or give your opinion of them unask'd also look not nigh when another is writing a Letter

Chapter ii. 28. C'est vne action directement opposée à la bienséance, de lire quelque livre, quelques lettres ou autres choses semblables dans vne conversation ordinaire, si ce n'est en vne affaire pressante, ou pour quelque peu de moments; & mesme encore en ce cas, est-il à propos d'en demander la permission, si vous n'estes, possible, le Superieur de la compagnie. C'est encore pis de manier les ouvrages des autres, leurs livres, & d'autres choses de cette nature, de s'y attacher, d'en approcher la veuë de plus prés, sans la permission de celuy à qui la chose appartient, aussi bien que de leur donner des loüanges, ou les censurer, auant que l'on vous en demande vostre sentiment; de s'approcher trop prés, & d'incommoder celuy de qui ou est voisin, lors qu'il prend la lecture de ses lettres ou de quelqu'-autre chose.

It is an act directly opposed to politeness to read a book, letters or anything else during ordinary conversation, if it be not a pressing matter, or only for a few moments, and even in that case it is proper to ask leave unless you are, possibly, the highest in rank of the company. It is even worse to handle other people's work, their books or other things of that nature, to go close to them, to look at them closely without the permission of the owner, and also to praise or find fault with them before your opinion has been asked; to come too close to any one near by, when he is reading his letters or anything else.

19th. let your Countenance be pleasant but in Serious Matters Somewhat grave

Chapter ii. 29. Que le visage ne paroisse point fantastique, changeant, égaré, rauy en admiration, couuert de tristesse, divers & volage, & ne fasse paroître aucun signe d'vn esprit inquiet: Au contraire, qu'il soil ouuert & tranquille, mais qu'il ne soit pas trop épanoüy de joye dans les affaires serieuses, ny trop retiré par vne grauité affectée dans la conversation ordinaire & familiere de la vie humaine.

The face should not look fantastic, changeable, absent, rapt in admiration, covered with sadness, various and volatile, and it should not show any signs of an unquiet mind. On the contrary, it should be open and tranquil, but not too expansive with joy in serious affairs, nor too self-contained by an affected gravity in the ordinary and familiar conversation of human life.

20th. The Gestures of the Body must be Suited to the discourse you are upon

Hawkins i. 30. Let the gestures of thy body, be agreeable to the matter of thy discourse. For it hath been ever held a solaesime in oratory, to poynt to the Earth, when thou talkest of Heaven.

(The nearest Maxim to this is one directed against excessive and awkward gesticulation in speaking, in which it is said: "Parmy les discours regardez à mettre vostre corps en belle posture" (While speaking be careful to assume an elegant posture).

21st. Reproach none for the Infirmaties of Nature, nor Delight to Put them that have in mind thereof.)

Chapter iv. 6. Ne reprochez les défauts à personne, non pas mesme de la nature, & ne prenez plaisir à faire confusion à qui que ce soit, par vos paroles.

Reproach none for their Infirmities—avoid it equally when they are natural ones—and do not take pleasure in uttering words that cause any one shame, whoever it may be.[16]

22d. Shew not yourself glad at the Misfortune of another though he were your enemy

Hawkins i. 32. When thou shalt heare the misfortunes of another, shew not thy selfe gladed for it, though it happ to thy enemy, for that will argue a mind mischievous, and will convict thee of a desire to have executed it thy selfe, had either power or opertunity seconded thy will.

(Nothing corresponding to Rule 22 is found among the Maxims of the Jesuit fathers; but the later French book has the following: "Shew not your self joyful and pleased at the misfortunes that have befallen another, though you hated him, it argues a mischievous mind, and that you had a desire to have done it your self, if you had had the power or opportunity to your will.")

23d. When you see a Crime punished, you may be inwardly Pleased; but always shew Pity to the Suffering Offender.

---

[16] Sidenote: Hawkins adds: "which by no Art can be amended."

Hawkins i. 33. When thou seest justice executed on any, thou maist inwardly take delight in his vigilancy, to punish offenders, because it tends to publique quiet, yet shew pity to the offender, and ever Constitute the defect of his morality, thy precaution.

[24th. Do not laugh too loud or] too much at any Publick [spectacle, lest you cause yourself to be laughed at.][17]

Hawkins i. 34. Laugh not too much or too Loud, in any publique spectacle least for thy so doing, thou present thy selfe, the only thing worthy to be laughed at.

25th. Superfluous Complements and all Affectation of Ceremony are to be avoided, yet where due they are not to be Neglected

Chapter iii. 1. Quoy qu'il soit bon de s'épargner vn trop grand soing de pratiquer vne ciuilité affectée, il faut pourtant estre exact à en obseruer ce qui est necessaire & auantageux pour faire paroistre une belle éducation, & ce qui ne se peut obmettre sans choquer ceux auec qui l'on converse.

Though it is right to avoid too great care in practising an affected civility, yet one must be exact in observing what is necessary and advantageous in order to show a good education, and all that cannot be omitted without shocking those with whom one is conversing.

26th. In pulling off your Hat to Persons of Distinction, as Noblemen, Justices, Churchmen, &c make a Reverence, bowing more or less according to the Custom of the Better Bred, and Quality of the Persons. Amongst your equals expect not always that they Should begin with you first, but to Pull off the Hat when there is no need is Affectation, in the Manner of Saluting and resaluting in words keep to the most usual Custom.

Chapter iii. 2. Témoignez vos respects aux hommes illustres & honorables, le chappeau en la main, comme aux Ecclesiastiques, ou aux Magistrats, ou à quelques autres personnes qualifiées; en tenant vers vous le dedans du chappeau que vous aurez osté: Faites leur aussi la reverence par quelque inclination de corps, autant que la dignité de chacun d'eux, & la belle coûtume des enfants bien nourris, le semble exiger. Et comme c'est vne chose fort inciuile de ne se pas découurir devant ceux à qui l'on doit ce respect, pour les saluër, ou d'attendre que vostre égal vous rend le premier ce deuoir; aussi de le faire, quand il

---

[17] Sidenote: This Rule has been nearly destroyed by mice.

n'est pas à propos, ressent sa ciuilité affectée: mais c'est vne honteuse impertinence de prendre garde si l'on vous rend vostre salutation. Au reste pour saluër quelqu'vn de parole, ce compliment semble le plus propre, qui est vsité par personnes le plus polies.

Show your respect for illustrious and honourable men,—such as Ecclesiastics, Magistrates, or other persons of quality,—hat in hand, holding the inside of the removed hat towards you; make your reverence to them by inclining your body as much as the dignity of each and the custom of well-bred youth seems to demand. And, as it is very rude not to uncover the head before those to whom one owes such respect, in order to salute them, or to wait till your equal should perform this duty towards you first, so also, to do it when it is not fitting savours of affected politeness: but it is shameful impertinence to be anxious for the return of one's salute. Finally, it seems most fitting to salute any one in words, a compliment which the politest persons are in the habit of using.

27th. Tis ill manners to bid one more eminent than yourself be covered as well as not to do it to whom it's due. Likewise he that makes too much haste to Put on his hat does not well, yet he ought to Put it on at the first, or at most the Second time of being ask'd; now what is herein Spoken, of Qualification in behaviour in Saluting, ought also to be observed in taking of Place, and Sitting down for ceremonies without Bounds is troublesome.

Chapter iii. 3. C'est une grande inciuilité d'entreprendre de prier vn superieur de se couurir, aussi bien que de n'en pas supplier celuy à qui cela se peut faire. Et celuy qui se haste trop de se couurir, particulierement en parlant à quelque personne qualifiée, ou qui pressé par plusieurs fois de ce faire, le refuse, choque la bienscéance; c'est pour cela qu'à la 1. ou 2. fois il est permis de se couurir, si l'vsage ne se trouue contraire en quelque Prouince ou Royaume. Et en effet entre les égaux, ou auec de plus âgez, soit Religieux, ou domestiques, il est permis d'accorder cette requeste à vn égal ou à vn plus ieune, dés la 1. fois. Toutefois ceux qui sõt égaux, ou fort péu differents les vns des autres, ont coustume de se faire cette priere, & de se couurir tout ensemble. Toutes les remarques donc qui se sont faites icy de la bonne conduite, doiuent estre aussi entenduës de l'ordre qu'il faut tenir à prendre place, & à s'asseoir: car le plaisir que l'on prend aux ciuilitez & aux complimens, est tout à fait importun.

It is very impolite to ask a superior to be covered, as it is not to do so in the case of one with regard to whom it is proper. And the man who is in haste to put his hat on, especially in talking to a person of quality, or who, having been urged several times to do so, refuses, shocks good manners; for this reason, after the first or second request, it is allowable to put the hat on, unless in some province or kingdom where the usage is otherwise. In fact, amongst equals, or with those who are older, or who belong to religious orders, or domestics, it is allowable to grant that request to one's equal or to a younger man, at the very first time. However, those of equal rank, or between whom there is little difference of rank, usually make the request and put on their hats at the same time. All the remarks here made on polite conduct, must also be extended to the order to be observed in taking places, and in sitting down; for the pleasure taken in ceremonies and compliments is really irksome.

28th. If any one come to Speak to you while you are Sitting Stand up tho he be your Inferiour, and when you Present Seats let it be to every one according to his Degree.

Chapter iii. 5. Si vous estes assis, lors que quelq'vn vous vient rendre visite, leuez-vous dés qu'il approche; si la dignité de la personne demande cette deference, comme s'il a quelque aduantage sur vous, s'il vous est égal, ou inferieur; mais non pas fort familier. Si vous vous reposez chez vous, ayant quelque siege, faites en soite de traiter chacun selon son merite.

If you are sitting down when any one pays you a call rise as soon as he comes near; whether his position demands that deference, as having precedence over you, or if he be your equal, or inferior; but not if he is on very intimate terms with you. If you are in your own house, having any seat to offer, manage to treat each guest according to his station.

29th. When you meet with one of Greater Quality than yourself, Stop, and retire especially if it be at a Door or any Straight place to give way for him to Pass

Chapter iii. 6. Quand vous rencontrez des personnes à qui vous deuez du respect, outre les devoirs d'vne salutation ordinaire, vous estes obligé de vous arrester quelque peu de temps, ou de rebrousser chemin jusqu'à l'entrée des portes, ou aux coins des rües, pour leur donner passage.

In meeting those to whom you should shew respect beyond the salutations which are their due, you should stop a little, or retreat to a threshold, or to the corner of the street, so as to make way for them.[18]

30th. In walking the highest Place in most Countrys Seems to be on the right hand therefore Place yourself on the left of him whom you desire to Honour: but if three walk together the middle Place is the most Honourable the wall is usually given to the most worthy if two walk together.

Chapter iii. 7. S'il arriue que vous faciez la promenade auec eux, vous leur laisserez tousiours la place honorable, qui est celle qui sera marquée par l'vsage. A parler generalement, il semble que plusieurs Nations ont passé en coustume que la droite soit tenuë pour vne marque de reuerence, de telle soit, que quand quelq'vn veut deferer à un autre, il le mette à sa droicte, en prenant sa gauche. Lors que trois hommes se promenent ensemble, le plus qualifié a tousiours le milieu: Celuy qui tient la droite, a le second lieu, & l'autre qui reste à la gauche, n'a que le troisiéme. Mais en France, quand l'on se promene au long d'vn mur; par ce que ce lieu est presque toujours plus eleué & plus net à cause de sa pente, la coûtume porte presque par tout qu'elle soit laissée au plus qualifié, & particulierement quand deux personnes marchent ensemble.

If you happen to take a walk with them, always give them the place of honour, which is that pointed out by usage. To speak generally, it appears that several nations have made it a custom that the right should always be held as a mark of esteem, so that, when any one wishes to honour another, he will put him on his right, himself taking the left. When three are walking together, he of the highest quality always has the middle: he who takes the right has the second place, and the other who remains on the left has the third. But in France, when walking by the side of a wall, that place being almost always higher and cleaner because of the slope, the custom almost always is that it be yielded to the man of the highest quality, and particularly when two are walking together.

31st. If any one far Surpasses others, either in age Estate, or Merit [yet, in any particular instance,] would give Place to a meaner than himself [in his own house or elsewhere] the one ought not to except it, So [the other, for fear of making him appear uncivil, ought not to press] it above once or twice.

---

[18] Sidenote: Walker says, "If you meet a superior in a narrow way, stop, and press to make him more room."

Chapter iii. 9. Si celuy qui se trouuera beaucoup plus avancé en âge, ou auantagé en dignité, soit en sa maison ou en quelqu'autre lieu, veut honorer son inferieur, comme il n'est pas à propos que cet inferieur s'en estime digne, de mesme aussi ne faut-il pas que celuy qui est superieur, l'en presse auec trop de soin, ou luy témoigne sa deference plus d'vne ou deux fois, de crainte que l'assiduité de sa supplication reïterée ne rabatte quelque chose de la bonne opinion que celuy qui le refuse, avoit conceu de son addresse & de sa courtoisie, ou qu'il luy fasse commettre enfin une inciuilité.

If he who is much the older, or has the advantage of rank, wishes, in his house or elsewhere, to honour his inferior, as it is not fitting that such inferior should think himself worthy, so also the superior must not press him too much or show such deference more than once or twice, lest the assiduity of his reiterated requests lower somewhat the good opinion which he who refuses, had conceived of his tact and courtesy, or lest, at last, it cause him to be guilty of some incivility.

32d. To one that is your equal, or not much inferior you are to give the chief Place in your Lodging and he to who 'tis offered ought at the first to refuse it but at the Second to accept though not without acknowledging his own unworthiness

Chapter iii. 10. Mais entre les égaux, il est bien à propos en receuant quelqu'vn dans sa maison, de luy donner la place la plus honnorable. Et celuy à qui l'on fait un sì bon accueil, en doit faire quelque refus d'abord, mais à la seconde instance de son amy, il luy doit obeyr.

But amongst equals, it is quite right, in receiving any one into one's house, to give him the most honourable place; and the person to whom one accords such a good reception ought at first rather to refuse it, but, when his friend insists a second time, he ought to obey him.[19]

33d. They that are in Dignity or in office have in all places Preceedency but whilst they are Young they ought to respect those that are their equals in Birth or other Qualitys, though they have no Publick charge.

---

[19] Sidenote: Maxim iii. 8, which says that acceptance of a first place should be accompanied by an acknowledgement of unworthiness, is represented in the last words of Rule 32.

Chapter iii. 12. A ceux qui out le cõmandement, & qui sont dans le pouuoir, ou qui exercent les Charges de Judicature, l'on donne tousiours les premieres places en toute sorte de compagnie. Mais qu'ils sçachent eux-mesmes que s'ils sont jeunes, ils sont obligez de respecter ceux qui sont d'aussi noble maison qu'eux, on qui les deuancent de beaucoup en âge, & sont honorez du degré de Doctorat; quoy qu'ils n'exercent aucune charge publique; Et bien plus, ils leur doiuent d'abord remettre la premiere place qu'il leur auoient deferé, & en suitte auec modestie, receuoir cest honneur comme une grace.

In every company the first place is always given to those in command, or in power, or who exercise judicial charges. But these, if young, should realise that they ought to respect those who belong to houses as noble as their own, or who are much older, and those honoured with the degree of Doctor, though not exercising any public function; and moreover they ought, at first, to return an offer of the highest place, and afterwards receive that honour modestly, as a favour.

34th. It is good Manners to prefer them to whom we speak before ourselves especially if they be above us with whom in no Sort we ought to begin.[20]

Chapter iii. 13. Il est de la derniere ciuilité de parler tousiours mieux de ceux auec qui nous avons à conuerser, que de vous mesmes: Et particulieremet quãd ce sont des personnes éleuées audessus de nous, auec qui il ne faut iamais contester en aucune maniere.

It is the height of politeness always to speak better of those with whom we have to converse than of ourselves. And particularly when they are persons of a superior rank to ourselves, with whom we ought never to dispute in any fashion.[21]

35th. Let your Discourse with Men of Business be Short and Comprehensive.

Chapter iii. 15. Le temps & le lieu, l'âge & la difference des personnes doivent regler tout cét vsage de compliments qui se fait parmy les plus polis, & particulierement ceux qui consistent dans les paroles. Mais l'on doit trancher court auec les personnes affairées & ne leur presenter plus aux nez toutes ses agreables fleurettes: il les faut épargner, & se faire entendre plustost par mines, qu'auec des paroles.

---

[20] Sidenote: The second clause is not in the French Maxims.
[21] Sidenote: Compare the last clause of this Maxim with Rule 40.

Time and place, age and the difference between persons, ought to regulate the whole custom of compliments as is done amongst the most polite, especially compliments that consist in words. But one should cut matters short with men of business, and not put one's fine flowerets under their nose; one should spare them, and make himself understood rather by looks than words.

36th. Artificers & Persons of low Degree ought not to use many ceremonies to Lords, or Others of high Degree but Respect and highly Honour them, and those of high Degree ought to treat them with affibility & Courtesie, without Arrogancy

Chapter iii. 16. Comme le soin de la ciuilité la plus raffinée ne doit pas beaucoup trauailler les esprits des Artisants & de la lie du peuple enuers les Grands & les Magistrats; aussi est-il raisonnable qu'ils ayent soin de leur rendre de l'honneur: de mesme il est à propos que la Noblesse les traitte [*sic*] doucement & les épargne, & qu'elle éuite toute sorte de superbe.

As the care for the most refined politeness ought not to trouble much the minds of artizans and of the dregs of the people, as regards Nobles and Magistrates, while it is reasonable that they should take care to honour such, so it is also right that the nobility should treat them gently, spare them, and avoid all manner of arrogance.

37th. In Speaking to men of Quality do not lean nor Look them full in the Face, nor approach too near them at lest Keep a full Pace from them.

Chapter iii. 18. En parlant aux personnes qualifiées, ne vous appuyez point le corps; ne leuez point vos yeux iusques sur leur visage; ne vous en approchez pas trop prés, & faites en sorte que ce ne soit iamais qu'à vn grãd pas de distance.

In speaking to persons of quality, do not lean your body on any thing; do not raise your eyes to their face; do not go too near, and manage to keep a full step from them.

38th. In visiting the Sick, do not Presently play the Physicion if you be not Knowing therein.

Chapter iii. 19. Quãd vous visiterez quelque malade, ne faites pas aussi-tost le Medicin, si vous n'estes point experimenté en cette science.

When you go to see any sick person do not immediately act the physician if you are not experienced in that science.

39th. In writing or Speaking, give to every Person his due Title According to his Degree & the Custom of the Place.

Chapter iii. 20. Lors que vous addresserez des lettres à des personnes qui seront dans l'estime publique; vous vous gouuernerez aupres d'eux, selon la coustume du pays & le degré de leur dignité. Quand vous aurez acheué vos lettres, relisez-les, pour en oster les fautes; mettez de la poudre sur l'escriture, lors qu'il en sera besoin & ne pliez iamais vostre papier que les characteres ne soient bien desechez, de crainte qu'ils ne s'effacent.

In addressing letters to persons held in public esteem, you will be regulated by the Customs of the country and the degree of their dignity. When you have finished your letters, read them over again so as to correct mistakes; sand the writing, when necessary, and never fold your paper until the letters are quite dry, lest they be effaced.

40th. Strive not with your Superiers in argument, but always Submit your Judgment to others with Modesty

Hawkins ii. 20. Strive not with thy Superiours, in argument or discourse, but alwayes submit thy opinion to their riper judgment, with modesty; since the possibility of Erring, doth rather accompany greene than gray hairs.

41st. Undertake not to teach your equal in the art himself Professes; it flavours of arrogancy.

Hawkins ii. 21. Doe not undertake to teach thy equal, in the Art himself professeth, for that will savour of Arrogancy, and serve for little other than to brand thy judgment with Rashnesse.

(*Nothing has been found in the French Maxims resembling Rule 41. Walker has the following*: "*Cautious also must be he who discourseth even of that he understands amongst persons of that profession: an affectation that more Scholars than wise men are guilty of; I mean to discourse with every man in his own faculty; except it be by asking questions and seeming to learn*" (*p. 266*)).

[42d. Let your ceremonies in] curtesie be proper to the Dignity of his place [with whom you converse; it is absurd to ac]t ye same with a Clown and a Prince.

Hawkins ii. 22. Let thy Seremonyes in Courtesy be proper to the dignity and place, of him with whom thou conversest. For it is absurd to honour a Clown with words courtly and of magnificence.

43d. Do not express Joy before one sick or in pain for that contrary Passion will aggravate his Misery

Hawkins ii. 23. Do not thou expresse joy before one sick, or in paine; for that contrary passion, will aggravate his misery. But do thou rather sympathize his infirmityes, for that will afford a gratefull easement, by a seeming participation.

44th. When a man does all he can though it Succeeds not well blame not him that did it.

Chapter iv. 3. Celui qui fait tout ce qui luy est possible, pour auancer vostre affaire, quoy qu'il ne la meine pas, & n'en puisse auoir le succez cõme vous l'esperez, ne doit point entendre de reprimãde; puis qu'il est plus digne de loüange que de blâme.

The man who does all he can to advance your business, even though he should not bring it about, and may not be able to obtain the success you hoped for, ought not to hear reproaches, since he is more worthy of praise than of blame.

45th. Being to advise or reprehend any one, consider whether it ought to be in publick or in Private; presently, or at Some other time in what terms to do it & in reproving Shew no signs of Cholar but do it with all Sweetness and Mildness[22]

Chapter iv. 4. Si vous auez à exhorter ou reprendre quelqu'vn, prenez bien garde, s'il est plus à propos de le faire en particulier ou en public, en ce temps ou en vn autre, bien plus, quelles paroles vous y deuez employer: Et particulierement lors que quelqu'vn ayãt esté desia reprimãdé d'autres fois, ne se corrige point des fautes passées, & ne promet point d'amandement. Et soit que vous donniez quelques auis, ou que vous fassiez quelque reprimande, donnez-vous de garde de vous mettre en cholere, au contraire pratiquez ces actions auec moderation & douceur.

---

[22] Sidenote: Hawkins has only 'sweetness,' Washington being here closer to the French.

If you have to exhort or to reproach any one, consider whether it be better to do so in private or in public; at this time or another and, above all, what words you should use: and particularly when some one having been already reprimanded at other times does not correct himself of his past faults, and does not promise any amendment. And if you give any advice, or impart any reprimand, carefully avoid anger; on the contrary, do such acts with moderation and sweetness.

46th. Take all Admonitions thankfully in what Time or Place Soever given but afterwards not being culpable take a Time or Place Convenient to let him know it that gave them.

Chapter iv. 5. Aussi quiconque se donnera la peine de vous remonstrer de quelque façõ, en quelque lieu, & en quelque temps qu'il le fasse, qu'il soit écouté de vostre part auec beaucoup de ressentiment de bienueillance & de reconnoissance. Et apres cela, si vous vous sentez innocent, & qu'il vous semble à propos de vous prouuer tel, il vous sera bien permis de le faire; mais auec ce soin de predre bien vostre temps, & plustost pour luy en faire voir la verité, & le tirer de peine, & plus si vous estes en sa charge, ou si vous releuez de son pouuoir, que pour vous appuyer de quelque excuse.

Also when any one takes the trouble to rebuke you, no matter how, where, or when he does it, hear him for your part with much feeling of goodwill and acknowledgment. And after that, if innocent, and it seems right to prove yourself so, you will be quite at liberty to do so; being careful, however, to choose a proper time, and rather to make him see the truth, and relieve him from anxiety,—the more if you are in his charge or depend on his authority—than to defend yourself with some excuse.

[4]7th. Mock not nor Jest at anything of Importance break no Jest that are Sharp Biting, and if you Deliver anything witty and Pleasent abtain from Laughing thereat yourself.

Chapter iv. 7. Ne vous amusez point aux equiuoques ny en matiere importante, ny en choses honteuses. Si vous trouuez bon de railler, gardez vous bien de mordre, & bien plus de déchirer comme un chien. Que les bons-mots & les rencontres soient tirées du suiet, que les vns & les autres ayent leur gentillesse & leur pointe, sans attirer l'indignation de personne. Que les plaisanteries ne soient point comme celles des bouffons, qui font rire par des representations extrauagantes, & des actions deshonnestes: si vous rencontrez ioliment, si vous donnez quelque bon-mot, en faisant rire les autres, empeschez-vous-en, le plus qu'il vous sera possible.

Do not divert yourself with *equivoques*, either in important or in mean matters. If you find good occasion for a joke, be careful not to bite, still less to tear, like a dog. Witticisms and repartee should be to the point, and should have elegance and appropriateness without exciting the indignation of any. Do not let your pleasantries degenerate into those of buffoons, who raise laughter by extravagant representations and indecent action. If you are clever in repartee, if you say a good thing, manage if possible, in making others laugh, to abstain from it yourself.

48th. Wherein wherein you reprove Another be unblameable yourself; for example is is more prevalent than Precepts

Hawkins iii. 8. Be sure thy conversation be in that poynt vertuous, wherein thou art desirous to retaine another, least thy Actions render thy advice unprofitable. Since the ratification of any advice is the serious prosecution of that vertue. For example hath ever been more prevalent than precept.

49th. Use no Reproachfull Language against any one neither Curse nor Revile

Hawkins iii. 11. Use no reproachfull language against any man, nor Curse, or Revile. For improperations and imprecations will rather betray thy affections than in any manner, hurt him against whom thou utters them.

[5]0th. Be not hasty to believe flying Reports to the Disparagement of any

Hawkins iii. 10. Thou oughtest not too suddenly to believe a flying Rumour of a friend, or any other. But let charity guid thy judgment, untill more certainty: for by this meanes thou securest his Reputation, and frees thy self of rashness.

51st. Wear not your Cloths, foul, unript or Dusty but See they be Brush'd once every day at least and take heed that you approach not to any Uncleanness

Chapter v. 4. Que vos habits ne demeurent point sales, déchirez, couuerts de poussiere, ou pelez. Qu'ils soient tous les iours du moins vne fois nettoyez auec les époussettes. Et prenez bien garde aussi en quel lieu vous vous assoirez, où vous vous mettrez à genoux, où vous vous accouderez, que le lieu ne soit point malpropre, ny reply d'immondices. Ne portez point le manteau sur le bras, à l'imitation des Fanfarons. Et mettant bas ou vostre robbe, ou vôtre mãteau, pliez les bien proprement & adroitement, & prenez bien garde où vous les posez.

Do not let your clothes be dirty, torn, covered with dust or threadbare. Have them brushed at least once a day. And take care also in what place you sit down, or kneel, or rest your elbows, that it be not unfit or filthy. Do not carry your cloak over your arm after the manner of swaggerers. And when you take off your coat or cloak, fold them neatly and carefully, and take care where you put them.

52nd. In your Apparel be Modest and endeavour to accomodate Nature, rather than to procure Admiration keep to the Fashion of your equals Such as are Civil and orderly with respect to Times and Places[23]

Chapter v. 5. Choisissez tousiours des habits semblables à ceux de vos compagnons qui passent pour les plus honnestes & moderez, en considerant les lieux & les temps auec discretion: & outre cela, faites qu'en ce poinct vous paroissiez souhaitter d'estre vestu le plus simplement & modestement de tous vos égaux, bien plustost que d'affecter les plus beaux vestements.

Always choose clothes like those of your companions who pass for the most genteel and moderate, in discreet consideration of time and place: and more, make it a point to be the most simply and modestly dressed of all your equals, rather than to affect the finest raiment.

53d. Run not in the Streets, neither go too slowly nor with Mouth open go not Shaking y'r Arms [stamping, or shuffling; nor pull up your stockings in the street. Walk] not upon the toes, nor in a Dancing [or skipping manner, nor yet with measured steps. Strike not the heels together, nor stoop when there is no occasion]

Chapter vi. 1. Faites en sorte quand vous marchez, de ne pas faire des démarches precipitées, d'auoir la bouche ouuerte & comme beante, & de ne vous trop demener le corps, ou le pancher, ou laisser vos mains pendantes, ou remuer & secoüer les bras; sans frapper trop rudement la terre, ou letter à vos pieds de part & d'autre. Cette sorte d'action demande encore ces conditions, que l'on ne s'arreste pas à retirer ses chausses en haut, dans le chemin, que l'on ne marche sur les extremitez des pieds, ny en sautillant ou s'eleuant, comme il se pratique en la dance, que l'on ne courbe point le corps, que l'on ne baisse point la

---

[23] Sidenote: 'Accomodate nature' is a phrase from a precept in Hawkins concerning apparel.

teste, qne l'on n'auance point à pas côptez, que l'on ne se choque point les talons l'un contre l'autre en entrant dans l'Eglise, que l'on ne reste point teste nuë a la sortie. Si la deuotion n'y oblige, comme lors qu'il est question d'accompagner le Tres-sainct Sacrement.

In walking guard against hurried steps, or having your mouth open and gaping; and do not move your body too much, or stoop, or let your hands hang down, or move and shake your arms; walk without striking the ground too hard or throwing your feet this way and that. That sort of action also demands these conditions,—not to stop to pull up one's stockings in the street, not to walk on the toes, or in a skipping rising as in dancing; do not stoop, nor bend the head; do not advance with measured steps; do not strike the heels against each other on entering church, nor leave it bareheaded, unless devotion requires it, as in accompanying the Holy Sacrament.

54th. Play not the Peacock, looking everywhere about you, to See if you be well Deck't, if your Shoes fit well if your Stockings Sit neatly, and Cloths handsomely.

Chapter vi. 2. Ne vous amusez pas à vous quarer comme vn Paon, & regarder superbement autour de vous, si vous estes bien mis, & bien chaussé, si vos hauts-dechausses & vos autres habits vous sont bienfaits. Ne sortez point de vostre châbre, portant vostre plume à vostre bouche, ou sur vostre aureille. Ne vous amusez pas à mettre des fleurs à vos aureilles, à vostre bonnet, ou à vostre chappeau. Ne tenez point vostre mouchoir à la main, ou pendu à vostre bouche, ny à vostre ceinture, ny sous vostre aiselle, ny sur vostre espaule, ou caché sous vostre robbe. Mettez-le en lieu d'où il ne puisse être veu, & il puisse estre toutesfois cõmodément tiré, dez qu'il en sera besoin. Ne le presentez iamais à personne, s'il n'est tout blanc, ou presque pas deployé.

Do not delight in strutting like a peacock, or look proudly around to see if you are well decked, if your breeches and other clothes fit well. Do not leave your room carrying your pen in your mouth or behind your ear. Do not indulge yourself by putting flowers in your ears, cap, or hat. Do not hold your pocket-handkerchief in your hand, hanging from your mouth, at your girdle, under your armpit, on your shoulder, or stuffed under your coat. Put it in some place where it cannot be seen, but from whence you may easily draw it when you want it. Never offer it to anybody unless it be quite clean, or hardly unfolded.

55th. Eat not in the Streets, nor in ye House, out of Season.

Chapter vi. 3. Ne marchez jamais par les chemins, en mangeant, soil seul ou en compagnie, & particulierement parmy la foule de la ville. Ne vous mettez pas mesme à manger en la maison hors de temps du repas, & du moins abstenez vous en, quand il s'y rencontrera quelqu'vn.

Never walk on the roads eating, whether alone or in company, especially amid the crowd in a town. Do not set to eating even in the house out of meal-times; at least abstain from it in the presence of others.

56th. Associate yourself with Men of good Quality if you Esteem your own Reputation; for 'tis better to be alone than in bad Company.

Chapter vi. 5. Et si, vous voulez passer pour honneste, accostez vous tousiours des Gents-de-bien, si vous n'en trouuez pas la commodité, ou par ce que vous n'en connoissez point, ou pour quelqu'autre raison, il vaut tousiours mieux que vous alliez seul, qu'en mauuaise compagnie.

If you wish to pass as genteel, always go with well-bred people; if you cannot get the chance,—from not knowing any, or any other reason,—it is always better to go alone than in bad company.

57th. In walking up and Down in a House, only with One in Company if he be Greater than yourself, at the first give him the Right hand and Stop not till he does and be not the first that turns, and when you do turn let it be with your face towards him, it he be a Man of Great Quality, walk not with him Cheek by Jowl but Somewhat behind him; but yet in such a Manner that he may easily Speak to you.

Chapter vi. 7. Si vous promenez auec vne personne seule dans la maison, & qu'il soil d'vne conditiõ qui luy fasse meriter quelque deference, dés le premier pas de la promenade, ne manquez pas de luy donner la droite: Ne cessez point de marcher, s'il ne vient à s'arrester: Ne changez pas le premier le diuertissement, & en vous tournant, ne luy montrez iamais les épaules; mais tousiours le visage. Si elle est dans vne charge releuée, gardez bien de marcher d'vn pas tout à fait égal; mais suiuez tant soit pen derriere, auec tant de iustesse pourtant & de moderatiõ, qu'elle vous puisse bien parler sans s'incõmoder. Si elle vous est égale allez d'un mesme pas tout le long de la promenade, & ne tournez pas tovsiours le premier, à chaque bout de champ; ne faites pas si souuent des pauses au milieu du chemin sans suiet. Car cette liberté ressent sa grandeur & donne du mécontentement. Celuy qui tient le milieu dans vne compagnie dont il est enuironné, si ceux qui la composent, sont égaux, ou presque égaux, il se doit tourner vne fois à droit dans la promenade, & s'ils se rencontrent notablement inegaux, il se doit plus souuent tourner vers le plus qualifié. Enfin que ceux qui l'enuironnent, viennent tousiours à se détourner de son costé & en mesme temps que luy, non point deuant ny apres; puis qu'il est comme le but de la promenade.[24]

If you are walking about the house alone with a person whose rank demands some deference, at the very first step be sure and give him the right hand: Do not stop walking if he does not wish to stop: Be not the first to change the diversion, and, in turning, never show him your shoulder but always your face. If he has a high public appointment take care not to walk quite side by side with him but a very little behind him with so much exactness and moderation that he may be able to speak to you without inconvenience. If he is your equal in rank, keep step with him during the whole walk, and do not always turn first at every end of the walk. Do not stop often midway without reason, such liberty touches his dignity and gives dissatisfaction. He who is the centre of the company by whom he is surrounded ought, if those of whom it consists are equal or nearly equal in rank, always to turn to the right once during the walk, and if they are manifestly unequal, he should oftenest turn towards the most distinguished. Lastly those who are about him should always turn round towards his side and at the same time as he, neither before nor after, as he is, so to say, the object of the walk.

58th. let your conversation be without malice or envy, for 'tis a sign of a tractable and commendable nature: & in all causes of passion admit reason to govern

Hawkins v. 9. Let thy conversation be without malice or envye, for that is a signe of a tractable and commendable nature. And in all causes of passion, admit reason for thy governesse. So shall thy Reputation be either altogether inviolable, or at the least not stayned with common Tinctures.

59th. Never express anything unbecoming, nor Act against the Rules Moral before your inferiours

---

[24] Sidenote: The repetition of the feminine "Elle" refers to 'vne personne,' in the first line, although the masculine ('qu'il' and 's'il') has twice followed it. There is no allusion to the female sex in the French Maxims.

Hawkins v. 10. Never expresse any thing unbeseeming, nor act against the Rules morall, before thy inferiours, For in these things, thy own guilt will multiply Crimes by example, and as it were, confirme Ill by authority.[25]

60th. Be not immodest in urging your Friends to Discover a Secret

Hawkins v. 11. Be not immodest in urging thy friend to discover his secrets; lest an accidentall discovery of them work a breach in your amitye.

61st. Utter not base and frivilous things amongst grave and Learn'd Men nor very Difficult Questions or Subjects, among the Ignorant or things hard to be believed, Stuff not your Discourse with Sentences amongst your Betters nor Equals[26]

Chapter vii. 1. dans la conuersation de gents doctes & habiles ne debitez pas des bagatelles, & n'auancez pas des discours trop releuez parmy les ignorants, qu'ils ne soient po[note: word missing here] capables d'entendre, ou qu'ils ne puissent pas croire fort facilement. ne debutez pas toûjours par des prouerbes, particulierement parmy vos égaux, & bien moins auec vos superieurs. ne parlez point de choses à côtrêteps, ou qui puissent choquer les esprits de vos auditeurs. parmy les banquets, & dans les iours de resioüissance ne mettez point sur le tapis de tristes nouuelles, point de recits de rudes calamitez, point d'ordures, point de deshônestetez, point d'afflictions. bien au côtraire si tels discours se trouuent entamez par quelqu'autre, faites vostre possible pour en détourner adroictement la suitte. ne contez iamais vos songes qu'à de vos confidents, & encore que ce soit pour profiter de leur interpretation; vous gardant bien d'y donner aucune croyance.

When talking with learned and clever men, do not introduce trifles, and do not bring forward too advanced conversation before ignorant people which they cannot understand nor easily believe. Do not always begin with proverbs, especially among your equals, and still less with your superiors. Do not speak of things out of place, or of such as may shock your hearers. At banquets and on days of rejoicing do not bring up sorrowful news or accounts of sad calamities, no filth, nothing improper, nothing afflicting. On the contrary, if such conversation is begun by any one else, do your best adroitly to turn the subject. Never relate your dreams except to your confidants, and then only to profit by

---

[25] Sidenote: Walker: 'A man should not divertise himself with his Inferiors, nor make his Servants privy to his infirmities and failures.'

[26] Sidenote: Hawkins uses the word 'Farce' instead of 'Stuff.'

their interpretation, taking care not to put the least belief in it.[27]

62d. Speak not of doleful Things in a Time of Mirth or at the Table; Speak not of Melancholy Things as Death and Wounds, and if others Mention them Change if you can the Discourse tell not your Dreams, but to your intimate Friend

(*The substance of Rule 62 is in the French Maxim quoted under the previous Rule (61), beginning with the third sentence, 'Ne parlez point, etc.'*)

63d. A Man ought not to value himself of his Atchievements or rare Qua[lities, his Riches, Tit]les Virtue or Kindred[; but he need not speak meanly of himself.]

Chapter vii. 2. Vne personne bien nourrie ne s'amuse iamais à faire parade de ses belles actions, de son esprit, de sa vertu, & de ses autres bonnes & loüables qualitez, au cõtraire il ne faut iamais s'entretenir auec les autres de sa haute naissance, ou de la Noblesse de ses parents, de ses richesses, ny de ses grandeurs, si l'on n'y est contrainct. Il ne faut pas aussi se raualler entierement.

A well-bred person never makes parade of his good actions, wit, virtue, and other good and praiseworthy qualities; on the contrary, one ought never to speak with another about his high birth, the nobility of his parents, his wealth or dignities, unless obliged to do so. But one need not efface himself altogether.

64th. Break not a Jest where none take pleasure in mirth Laugh not aloud, nor at all without Occasion, deride no man's Misfortune, tho' there seem to be Some cause

Chapter vii. 3. Il ne faut pas se mettre sur la raillerie, quãd il n'est point temps de solastrer. Gardez-vous bien d'éclater en risées, d'y passer les bornes de la bienseance, & de le faire sans un suiet raisonnable, pour suiure l'inclinatiõ qui vous porte à rire. Ne prenez iamais suiet de rire du malheur d'autruy, quoy qu'il semble en quelque façon digne de risée.

---

[27] Sidenote: Walker says—'nor tell your dreams when perhaps your best waking actions are not worth the reciting.'

Jesting must be avoided when it is out of season. Beware of bursting out into laughter, beyond the limits of decorum, and of doing so without reasonable cause, merely from an inclination to laugh. Never laugh at the misfortunes of others, although they seem in some sort laughable

65th. Speak not injurious Words neither in Jest nor Earnest Scoff at none although they give Occasion

Chapter vii. 4. Ne donnez iamais de sobriquet, soit dans le jeu, ou bien hors du jeu. Gardez vous bien de picquer qui que ce puisse estre; ne vous mocquez d'aucune personne, particulierement d'entre celles qui sont qualifiées, quoy qu'auec occasion.

Never give nicknames, whether in fun or not. Take care not to hurt anybody, whoever it may be; do not mock any one, especially persons of distinction, although there be occasion.

66th. Be not forward but friendly and Courteous; the first to Salute hear and answer & be not Pensive when it's a time to converse.

Chapter vii. 5. Ne vous rendez point morne & de fâcheux abord; mais affable & prompt à rendre de bons offices, & soyez toûjours le premier à saluër. Entendez bien ce que l'on vous dit & y respondez; Ne vous retirez point à l'écart, quand le deuoir vous engage à la conversation.

Do not be glum and unfriendly of approach; but affable, prompt in rendering kind offices, and always the first to salute. Listen carefully to what is said and respond; do not keep aloof when duty requires you to take a share in the conversation.

67th. Detract not from others neither be excessive in Commending.

Chapter vii. 6. Gardez vous bien de medire d'aucune personne ou de vous entretenir des affaires d'autruy. Et mesme souuenez vous de garder la moderation dans vos loüanges.

Take care not to speak ill of any one or to gossip of other people's affairs. At the same time do not forget moderation in your praises.[28]

---

[28] Sidenote: Walker says: 'Carry even between adulation and soureness.'

(*Dr. Toner thinks the last word of Rule 67 is written 'Commanding.' Sparks has 'commending.'*)

68th. Go not thither, where you know not, whether you Shall be Welcome or not. Give not Advice whth being Ask'd & when desired do it briefly

Chapter vii. 7. Ne vous ingerez pas dans les entretiens & les consultations, où vous ne serez pas asseuré d'estre le bien venu. Ne dites iamais vostre aduis des affaires que l'on ne vous l'ait demandé, si toutesfois vous n'estes le premier en authorité, & que ce ne soit point à contre-temps, ou sans apparence de quelque auantage. Quand vous en estes prié, abregez vostre discours, & prenez de bonne heure le noeud de l'affaire à demesler.

Do not force yourself into interviews or consultations at which you are not sure of being welcome. Never give your advice on matters when it has not been asked, unless you happen to be the highest in authority; and do not let it be done out of place or without prospect of any benefit. When your opinion is requested, be brief, and reach quickly the knot of the matter under discussion.

69th. If two contend together take not the part of either unconstrained, and be not obstinate in your Opinion, in Things indiferent be of the Major side.

Chapter vii. 8. Si deux personnes out quelque chose à decider ensemble, ne prenez le party ny de l'vn, ny de l'autre, si quelque grãde raison ne vous y oblige. Ne soustenez pas vos sentiments auec vne trop grande obstination. Dans les matieres où les opiniõs sont libres, prenez tousiours le party qui est le plus appuyé.

If two persons have anything to decide between themselves do not take the part of either unless some pressing reason obliges you to do so. Do not maintain your ideas too obstinately. In matters in which opinions are free, always take the side which has the most support.[29]

70th. Reprehend not the imperfections of others for that belongs to Parents Masters and Superiors.

---

[29] Sidenote: Walker says: 'Thrust not your self to be Moderator or Umpire in Controversies, till required.'

Chapter vii. 9. Ne faites pas le censeur & le juge des fautes d'autruy, car cela n'appartient qu'aux maistres, aux peres, & à ceux qui out quelque superiorité. Il vous est toutesfois permis de faire paroistre l'auersion que vous en côceuez. Et vous pouuez bien quelquesfois dôner aduis avantageux au defaillants.

Do not be the censor and judge of other peoples' faults, for that only belongs to masters, fathers, and those who have some superiority. But it is nevertheless allowable for you to show an aversion you have conceived. And at times you may give advantageous advice to those who are in the wrong.

71st. Gaze not at the marks or blemishes of Others and ask not how they came. What you may Speak in Secret to your Friend deliver not before others

Chapter vii. 10. Ne vous amusez pas à considerer curieusement les defauts ou les taches, quoy que naturelles, particulierement si elles se rencontrent au visage, & ne vous enquerez pas d'où elles out precedé. Ce que vous diriez bien volontiers en l'oreille à vn amy, doit estre conserué sous la clef du silêce, lors que vous vous trouuez en cempagnie

Take no pleasure in examining curiously defects or blemishes, although natural, especially if they be in the face, nor enquire what they proceed from. What you would readily say in the ear of a friend ought to be preserved under the key of silence when you are in society.

72d. Speak not in an unknown Tongue in Company but in your own Language and that as those of Quality do and not as y'e Vulgar; Sublime matters treat Seriously.

Chapter vii. 11. Ne vous seruez iamais en vos discours & n'employez vne langue qui ne vous est pas bien cognuë & familiere, si ce n'est en vne occasion bien pressante, pour donner plus clairement à connoistre vostre pensée. Parlez tousiours en la vostre maternelle & natale, non pas grossierement, comme la lie du peuple, ou les pauures chambrieres; mais comme les plus delicats & les plus gros Bourgeois, auec erudition & auec elegance. Et prenez à tâche d'obseruer en vos discours les regles de l'honnesteté & de la modestie; & vous gardez bien de ces contes vn peu trop libres; ne les faites ny en l'oreille d'vn autre, ny ne les poussez par jeu auec profusion. N'employez point de termes bas & raualez ou populaires en des matieres hautes & reluées.

In your conversation never use a language with which you are not thoroughly acquainted and familiar, unless in some very urgent case to render your idea more clearly. Always speak in your native and mother tongue, not coarsely like the dregs of the people, or poor chambermaids, but like the most refined and well-to-do citizens, with erudition and elegance. And in your discourse take care to observe the rules of decorum and modesty, and be sure to avoid rather risky tales; do not whisper such to another, and do not indulge them too frequently in sport. Do not use low, base or vulgar expressions when treating of serious and sublime subjects.

73d. Think before you Speak pronounce not imperfectly nor bring out your Words too hastily but orderly and Distinctly

Chapter vii. 12. Ne vous mettez point à discourir, que vous ne vous y soyez bien preparé, & que vous n'ayez bien estudié vostre suiet. Dans l'entretien ordinaire, n'allez point chercher de periphrases, point de subtilitez, ny de figures. Ne confondez point vos paroles dans les coutumes d'vne langue trop brusque & begayante; mais aussi, ne parlez pas si lentement, & à tant de reprises, que vous donniez de l'ennuy.

Do not begin speaking unless you are quite prepared, and have well studied your subject. In ordinary conversation do not seek periphrases, subtleties, or figures of speech. Do not let your words become confused by too abrupt or hesitating a delivery, and do not let your speech be so slow and broken as to become tedious.

74th. When Another Speaks be attentive your Self and disturb not the Audience if any hesitate in his Words help him not nor Prompt him without desired, Interrupt him not, nor Answer him till his Speech be ended[30]

Chapter vii. 13. Quand quelque autre parle, prenez garde de donner suiet à ses Auditeurs de s'en detourner; & pour vous, écoutez-le fauorablement & auec attention, sans destourner les yeux d'vn autre costé, ou vous arrester à quelqu'autre pensée. Si quelqu'vn a de la peine à tirer ses mots comme par force, ne vous amusez pas á luy en suggerer, pour faire paroistre quelque desir d'aider celuy qui parle, si'l ne vient à vous en prier, ou que le tout se passe dãs le particulier, & qu'encore cette persõne soit de vos plus intimes & familiers amis; & apres tout ne l'interrompez point, & ne luy repliquez en aucune maniere, iusques à ce que luy-mesme ait acheué.

---

[30] Sidenote: Hawkins: 'If any drawl forth his words, help him not.'

When another person is speaking, beware of drawing off the attention of his hearers; and as for yourself, listen to him favourably and attentively, without turning your eyes aside or directing your thoughts elsewhere. If any one finds difficulty in expressing himself, do not amuse yourself by suggesting words to him, so as to show a desire to assist the speaker unless he so requests or you are quite in private, and the person is also one of your most intimate and familiar friends. Above all, do not interrupt him, and in nowise reply to him until he has finished.[31]

75th. In the midst of Discourse ask [not what it is about], but if you Perceive any Stop because of [your arrival, rather request the speaker] to Proceed: If a Person of Quality comes in while your Conversing its handsome to Repeat what was said before

Chapter vii. 14. Quand vous arriuez sur la moitié de quelque discours, ne vous enquerez pas du suiet de l'entretien; car cela est trop hardy & ressent l'homme d'authorité. Suppliez plûtost honnestement & courtoisement que l'on le poursuiue, si vous voyez qu'il se soir interronpu à vostre arriuée, parquel que sorte de deference. Au contraire s'il suruient quelqu'vn, lors que vous parlerez, & particulierement si c'est vne personne qualifiée & de merite, il est de la bien-seance de faire vne petite recapitulation de ce qui a esté auancé, & de poursuiure la deduction de tout le reste de la matiere.

If you arrive in the middle of any discussion, do not ask what it is about; for that is too bold and savours of one in authority. Rather ask, genteelly and courteously, that it may be continued, if you see that the speaker has paused on your arrival, out of civility. On the other hand, if any one comes whilst you are speaking, and particularly if it be a person of quality or of merit, it is in accordance with good manners to give a slight recapitulation of what has been advanced, and then carry out the deduction of all the rest of the matter.[32]

76th. While you are talking, Point not with your Finger at him of Whom you Discourse nor Approach too near him to whom you talk especially to his face

---

[31] Sidenote: The later French book has: 'It is not Civil when a Person of Quality hesitates or stops in his discourse for you to strike in, though with pretence of helping his memory.'

[32] Sidenote: Hawkins: 'It is seemely to make a little Epilogue and briefe collection of what thou deliveredst.'

Chapter vi. 17. Ne montrez point au doigt la personne dont vous parlez, & ne vous approchez point trop prés de celuy que vous entretenez, non plus que de son visage, à qui il faut toûjours porter quelque reuerence.

Do not point your finger at the person of whom you are speaking, and do not go too near any one with whom you are conversing, especially not near his face, which should always be held in some reverence.

77th. Treat with men at fit Times about Business & Whisper not in the Company of Others

Chapter vi. 18. Si vous auez vne affaire particuliere à communiquer a l'vne de deux personnes ou de plusieurs qui s'entretiennent ensemble, expediez en trois mots, & ne luy dites pas en l'oreille ce que vous auez à proposer; mais si la chose est secrette, tirez-la tant soit peu à l'écart, s'il vous est possible, & que rien ne vous en empesche; parlez luy en la langue que les assistants entendent.

If you have any particular matter to communicate to one of two persons or of several, who are talking together, finish it off in three words, and do not whisper in his ear what you have to say; if the matter be secret, take him aside a little, if possible, and nothing prevents; speak to him in the language which those present understand.

78th. Make no Comparisons and if any of the Company be Commended for any brave act of Virtue, commend not another for the Same

Chapter vii. 21. Abstenez vous de faire des comparaisons des personnes l'vne auec l'autre; Et partant si l'on donne des loüanges à quelqu'vn pour vne bonne action, ou pour sa vertu, gardez vous bien de loüer la mesme vertu en quelque autre. Car toute comparaison se trouue odieuse.

Abstain from drawing comparisons between different persons; and if any one is praised for a good action, or for his virtue, do not praise another for the same. For all comparisons are odious.

79th. Be not apt to relate News if you know not the truth thereof. In Discoursing of things you Have heard Name not your Author always A Secret Discover not

Chapter vii. 22. Ne faites pas aisément dessein de redire aux autres les nouuelles & les rapports qui auront couru touchant les rencontres des affaires, si vous n'auez vn garant de leur verité. Et ne vous amusez pas en racontant ces vau-de-villes, d'en citer l'Autheur, que vous ne soyez bien asseuré qu'il ne le trouuera pas mauuais. Gardez tousiours bien le secret qui vous a esté confié & ne le ditez à personne, de crainte qu'il ne soit diuulgué.

Be not apt to relate rumours of events, if you know not their truth. And in repeating such things do not mention your authority, unless you are sure he will like it. Always keep the secret confided to you; tell it to no one, lest it be divulged.[33]

80th. Be not Tedious in Discourse or in reading unless you find the Company pleased therewith

Chapter vii. 23. Si vous racontez, ou lisez, ou entreprenez d'en prouuer par raisonnements quoy que ce soit, tranchez-le-court, & particulierement quand le suiet en est peu important, ou quand vous reconnoissez les dégousts qu'en ont les Auditeurs.

If you are relating or reading anything, or arguing any point, be brief,—particularly when the subject is of small importance, or if you detect weariness in the listeners.

81st. Be not Curious to Know the Affairs of Others neither approach to those that Speak in Private

Chapter vii. 24. Ne témoignez pas de curiosité dans les affaires d'autruy, & ne vous approchez dé là où l'on parle en secret.

Do not show any curiosity about other people's affairs, and do not go near the place where persons are talking in private.

82d. Undertake not what you cannot Perform but be Carefull to keep your Promise

Chapter vii. 25. Ne vous chargez point d'vne chose dont vous ne vous pouuez acquiter; maintenez ce que vous auez promis.

Do not undertake anything that you cannot perform; keep your promise.

---

[33] Sidenote: The later French book says: 'Discover not the secret of a friend, it argues a shallow understanding and a weakness.'

83d. When you deliver a matter do it without Passion & with Discretion, however mean y'e Person be you do it too

Chapter vii. 27. Quand vous faites vne ambassade, vn rapport, ou donnez l'ouuerture de quelque affaire, taschez de le faire sans passion & auec discretion, soit que vous ayez à traitter auec personnes de peu, ou personnes de qualité.

When you fulfil a mission, deliver a report, or undertake the opening of any matter, try to do it dispassionately and discreetly, whether those with whom you have to treat be of humble or high position.

84th. When your Superiours talk to any Body hearken not neither Speak nor Laugh

Chapter vii. 27. Quand ceux qui out sur vous commandement, parlent à quelqu'vn, gardez vous bien de parler, de rire, ou de les escouter.

When your Superiors talk to any one, do not speak, laugh, or listen.

85th. In Company of these of Higher Quality than yourself Speak not till you are ask'd a Question then Stand upright put of your Hat & Answer in few words

Chapter vii. 30. Estant auec de plus grands que vous, principalement s'ils ont du pouuoir sur vous, ne parlez pas deuant que d'estre interrogé, & alors leuez-vous debout, découurez-vous, & répondez en pen de mots, si toutesfois l'on ne vous donne congé de vous asseoir, ou de vous tenir couuert.

Being with persons of higher position than yourself, and especially if they have authority over you, do not speak until you are interrogated; then rise, remove your hat, and answer in few words,—unless indeed you are invited to remain seated, or to keep your hat on.

86th. In Disputes, be not so Desirous to Overcome as not to give Liberty to each one to deliver his Opinion and Submit to y'e Judgment of y'e Major Part especially if they are Judges of the Dispute.

Chapter vii. 31. Dans les disputes qui arriuent, principalement en conuersation, ne soyez pas si desireux de gagner, que vous ne laissiez dire a chacun son aduis, & soit que vous ayez tort, ou raison, vous deuez acquiescer au jugement du plus grand nombre, ou mesme des plus fascheux, & beaucoup plus de ceux de qui vous dépendez, ou qui sont juges de la dispute.

In disputes that arise, especially in conversation, be not so desirous to overcome as not to leave each one liberty to deliver his opinion; and whether you be wrong or right you should acquiesce in the judgment of the majority, or even of the most persistent, all the more if they are your masters or patrons, or judges of the discussion.

87th. [Let your bearing be such] as becomes a Man Grave Settled and attentive [to what is said, without being too serious. Contra]dict not at every turn what others Say

Chapter vii. 35. Vostre maintien soit d'homme modérément graue, posé, & attentif a ce qui se dit, afin de n'auoir pas à dire à tout propos: *Comment ditez-vous? comment se passe cela? je ne vous ay pas entendu*, & d'autres semblables niaiseries.
33. Ne contredictes pas a tout bout de champ, à ce que disent les autres, en contestant & disant: Il n'est pas ainsi, la chose est comme je la dy; mais rapportez-vous en à l'opinion des autres principalement dans les choses, qui sont de peu de consequence.

35. Let your bearing be that of a moderately grave, serious man, and attentive to what is said so as to avoid having to say every moment: '*How did that happen? I did not understand you,*'—and other similar foolish remarks.
33. Do not continually contradict what others say, by disputing and saying: 'That is not the case, it is as I say;' but defer to the opinion of others, especially in matters of small consequence.

88th. Be not tedious in Discourse, make not many Digressions, nor repeat often the Same manner of Discourse

Chapter vii. 39. N'employez pas vn an à vostre preface, & en certaines longues excuses ou ceremonies, en disant, *Monsieur: excusez-moy! si ie ne sçay pas si bien dire*, &c., *toutesfois pour vous obeyr*, &c., & autres semblables ennuyeuses and sottes trainées de paroles; mais entrez promptement en matiere tant que faire se pourra auec vne hardiesse moderée: Et puis poursuiuez, sans vous troubler, iusques à la fin. Ne soyez pas long; sans beaucoup de digressions, ne reïterez pas souuent vne mesme façon de dire.

Do not take a year in your preface, or in certain long apologies or ceremonies, such as: '*Pardon me Sir if I do not know how to express myself sufficiently well,* &.c.; *nevertheless in order to obey you,*' &c., and other similarly tedious and stupid circumlocutions; but enter promptly on the subject, as far as possible, with moderate boldness; then continue to the end without hesitation. Do not be prolix; avoid digressions; do not often reiterate the same expression.

89th. Speak not Evil of the absent for it is unjust

Hawkins vi. 40. Speak not evill of one absent, for it is unjust to detract from the worth of any, or besmeare a good name by condemning, where the party is not present, to clear himselfe, or undergo a rationall conviction.

90th. Being Set at meat Scratch not neither Spit Cough or blow your Nose except there's a Necessity for it

Chapter viii. 2. Estant assis à table, ne vous grattez point, & vous gardez tant que vous pourrez, de cracher, de tousser, de vous moucher: que s'il y a necessité, faites-le adroitement, sans beaucoup de bruit, en tournant le visage de costé.

Being seated at the table, do not scratch yourself, and if you can help it, do not spit, cough, or blow your nose; should either be necessary do it adroitly, with least noise, turning the face aside.

(*In the Washington MS. there is a notable omission of all that is said in the French and English books concerning grace before meat. At Washington's table grace was never said.*)

91st. Make no Shew of taking great Delight in your Victuals, Feed not with Greediness; cut your Bread with a Knife, lean not on the Table neither find fault with what you Eat.

Chapter viii. 3. Ne prenez pas vostre repas en gourmand.
4. Ne rompez point le pain auec les mains, mais auec le cousteau, si ce n'estoit vn pain fort petil & tout frais, & que tous les autres fissent de mesme, ou la pluspart.
5. Ne vous iettez pas sur table, à bras estendus iusques aux coudes, & ne vous accostez pas indecemment les épaules ou les bras sur vostre siege.
8. Ne monstrez nullement d'avoir pris plaisir à la viande, ou au vin; mais si celuy que vous traittez, vous en demande vostre goust,

vous pourrez luy respondre avec modestie & prudence: beaucoup moins faut il blasmer les viandes, ou en demander d'autres, ny dauantage.

3. Eat not like a glutton. (4.) Do not break the bread with your hands, but with a knife; unless, indeed, it is a small and quite fresh roll, and where the others present, or most of them, use their hands. (5.) Do not throw yourself on the table, as far as the elbows, nor unbecomingly rest shoulders or arms on your chair. (8.) Do not make a show of taking delight in your food, or in the wine; but if your host inquires your preference you should answer with modesty and tact: whatever you do, do not complain of the dishes, ask for others, or anything of that sort.

(*At Washington's table it was a custom to invite each guest to call for the wine he preferred.*)

92d. Take no Salt or cut Bread with your Knife Greasy.

Chapter viii. 9. Prenant du sel, gardez que le cousteau ne soit gras: quand il le faut nettoyer, ou la fourchette on le peut faire honnestement auec vn peu de pain, ou comme il se pratique en certains lieux, auec la serviette, mais iamais sur le pain entier.

In taking salt be careful that the knife is not greasy: when necessary your knife or fork may with propriety be cleaned on a piece of bread,—or, as is done in some places, with the napkin,—but it must never be wiped on the whole loaf.

93d. Entertaining any one at table it is decent to present him w't meat, Undertake not to help others undesired by y'e Master

Chapter viii. 10. Traittant quelqu'vn, il est de la bien-seance de le seruir en table, & luy presenter des viandes, voire mesme de celles qui sont proches de luy. Que si l'on estoit invité chez autruy, il est plus à propos d'attendre que le Maistre ou vn autre serue, que de prendre des viandes soy-mesme, si ce n'estoit que le Maistre priast les conuiez de prendre librement, ou que l'on fust en maison familiere. L'on se doit aussi peu ingerer à seruir les autres hors de sa maison, où l'on avoir peu de pouuoir, n'étoit que le nombre des conuiez fust grand, & que le Maistre de la maison ne peust pas avoir l'oeil sur tout; Et pour lors l'on peut seruir ceux qui sont proches de soy.

When entertaining any one it is polite to serve him at table and to present the dishes to him, even such as are near him. When invited by another it is more seemly to wait to be served by the host, or some one else, than to take the dishes oneself, unless the host begs the guests to help themselves freely, or one is at home in the house. One ought also not to be officious in helping others when out of one's own house, where one has but little authority, unless the guests are very numerous and the host cannot attend to everything; in that case we may help those nearest us.

[9]4th. If you Soak bread in the Sauce let it be no more than what you put in your Mouth at a time and blow not your broth at Table but Stay till Cools of it Self

Chapter viii. 14. Si vous trempez en la saulce le pain ou la chair, ne les trempez pas derechef, apres y auoir mordu, trempez-y à chaque fois vn morceau mediocre, qui se puisse manger tout d'vne bouchée.
11. Ne soufflez point sur les viandes; mais si elles sont chaudes, attendez qu'elles se refroidissent: le potage se pourra refroidir, le remuant modestement auec la cuilliere, mais il ne sied pas bien de humer son potage en table, il le faut prendre auec la cuilliere.

If you dip bread or meat into the gravy, do not do so immediately after biting a piece off, but dip each time a moderately-sized morsel which can be eaten at one mouthful. (11.) Do not blow on the viands, but if they are hot, wait till they cool. Soup may be cooled by stirring it gently with a spoon, but it is not becoming to drink up the soup at table. It should be taken with a spoon.

95th. Put not your meat to your Mouth with your Knife in your hand neither Spit forth the Stones of any fruit Pye upon a Dish nor cast anything under the table

Chapter viii. 17. Ne portez pas le morceau à la bouche, tenant le cousteau en la main, à la mode des villageois.
16. Aussi ne semble-il bien seant de cracher les noyaux de prunes, cerises, ou autre chose semblable sur le plat; mais premierement on doit les recueiller decemment, comme il a esté dit, en la main gauche, l'approchant à la bouche, & puis les mettre sur le bord de l'assiette.
15. L'on ne doit point jetter sous la table, ou par terre, les os, les écorces, le vin ou autre chose semblable.[34]

---

[34] Sidenote: Maxim 15 is much longer.

Do not carry a morsel to your mouth, knife in hand, like the rustics. (16.) Moreover, it does not seem well bred to spit out the kernels of prunes, cherries, or anything of the kind, on your plate, but, as already said, they should be decently collected in the left hand (raised to the mouth), and placed on the edge of the plate. (15.) Bones, peel, wine, and the like, should not be thrown under the table.

96th. Its unbecoming to Stoop much to one's Meat Keep your Fingers clean & when foul wipe them on a Corner of your Table Napkin.

Chapter viii. 21. Il est messeant de se baisser beaucoup sur son escuelle ou sur la viande, c'est assez de s'encliner vn peu lors que l'on porte le morceau trempé à la bouche, de crainte de se salir, & puis redresser la teste.

25. Ne vous nettoyez pas les mains à vostre pain, s'il est entier; toutesfois les ayant fort grasses, il semble que vous les puissiez nettoyer premierement à vn morceau de pain que vous ayez à manger tout à l'heure & puis à la seruiette, afin de ne la point tant salir: ce qui vous arriuera rarement, si vous sçauez vous seruir de la cuilliere, & de la fourchette, selon le style des plus honnestes. Beaucoup moins deuez vous lêcher les doigts, principalement les sucçant auec grand bruit.

It is ill-bred to stoop too close to one's porringer or the meat. It suffices to bend a little when conveying a soaked morsel to one's mouth, in order to avoid soiling oneself, then straighten up again. (25.) Do not clean your hands on a loaf; if very greasy you might, it would seem, partly clean them on a bit of bread you are about to eat, then on your napkin, so as not to soil the latter too much: this will rarely happen if you know how to use spoon and fork in the most approved manner. Much less should you lick your fingers, especially not suck them noisily.

[9]7th. Put not another bit into your Mouth till the former be Swallowed let not your Morsels be too big for the jowls

Chapter viii. 30. Ne portez pas le morceau à la bouche que l'autre ne soil auallé, & que tous soient tels qu'ils ne fassent pas enfler les jouës hors de mesure; ne vous seruez pas des deux mains pour vous mettre le morceau à la bouche, mais seruez vous d'ordinaire de la droite.

Carry not another morsel to the mouth till the other be swallowed, and let each be such as will not stretch the jaws beyond measure; do not take both hands to raise a morsel to the mouth, but, usually, serve yourself with the right hand.

98th. Drink not nor talk with your mouth full neither Gaze about you while you are a Drinking

Chapter viii. 32. Ne boiuez ayant le morceau en la bouche, ne demandez point à boire, ne parlez, ne vous versez point à boire, & ne boiuez cependant que vostre voisin boit, ou celuy qui est au haut bout.
33. En boiuant, ne regardez point çà & là.

Do not drink with your mouth full of food; do not ask anything while drinking, nor talk, nor turn round; and do not drink because your neighbour does, or the head of the table. (33.) While drinking, gaze not here and there.[35]

99th. Drink not too leisurely nor yet too hastily. Before and after Drinking wipe your Lips breath not then or Ever with too Great a Noise, for its uncivil

Chapter viii. 34. Ne boiuez point trop lentement ny trop à la haste, ny comme en maschant le vin, ny trop souuent ny sans eau, car c'est à faire aux yvrognes. Deuant & apres que vous aurez beu, effuyez-vous les lévres, & ne respirez pas auec trop grand bruit, ny alors, ny iamais, car c'est vne chose bien inciuile.

Drink neither too slowly nor too hastily, nor as if gulping the wine, nor too frequently, nor without water—as drunkards do. Wipe your lips before and after drinking, and do not breathe too loudly then or at any other time, for that is very inelegant.

100th. Cleanse not your teeth with the Table Cloth Napkin Fork or Knife but if Others do it let it be done w't a Pick Tooth

Chapter viii. 36. Ne vous nettoyez pas les dents auec la nappe, ou la seruiette, ny auec le doigt, la fourchette, ou le cousteau. Ce seroit faire pis de le faire auec les ongles, mais faites-le auec le curedent. Aussi ne semble-il estre bien-seant de se les nettoyer en table, si ce n'estoit que les autres le fissent, & que ce fust la coustume des mieux ciuilisez.

---

[35] Sidenote: The later French book recommends keeping the eyes 'fixed at the bottom of the glass' while drinking.

Do not clean your teeth with the tablecloth, napkin, finger, fork, or knife. It were still more objectionable to do so with the nails. Use a toothpick. It also does not appear well-bred to pick them at table, unless others do so, and where such is a custom of the more gentlemanly.

101st. Rince not your Mouth in the Presence of Others

Chapter viii. 37. Ne vous rincez point la bouche auec du vin, pour le reietter en presence des autres; mais sorty que vous serez de table, accoustumez vous à lauer les mains auec les autres. Quant à la bouche, il semble n'estre pas à propos de la lauer en presence des gens, & partant quand l'on donne à lauer, mesme en table, l'on doit seulement lauer les mains.

Do not rinse your mouth with wine, to be rejected in the presence of others; but, having left the table, accustom yourself to wash your hands with the rest. As to the mouth, it does not appear proper to wash it in company at all, and consequently when an opportunity of washing is offered, even at the table, the hands only should be washed.

102d. It is out of use to call upon the Company often to Eat nor need you Drink to others every Time you Drink

Chapter viii. 38. C'est chose peu loüable & presque aujourd'huy hors d'vsage, d'inuiter la compagnie à manger, principalement trop souuent & auec importunité, car il semble qu'on luy osté la liberté. Beaucoup moins deuez-vous boire à autruy toutes les fois que vous boiuez: que si l'on boit à vous, vous pouuez le refuser modestement, remerciant de bonne grace, & confessant de vous rendre; ou bien essayez vn peu le vin par courtoisie, principalement auec gens qui sont accoustumez. à cela, & prennent le refus à iniure.

It is not commendable, and now almost out of fashion, to call on the company to eat, especially to invite them too often and urgently, for it appears to take away their freedom. Much less should you drink to others every time you drink: if one drinks to you, it is permissible to decline modestly, thanking him gracefully, and acknowledging your response; or you may well sip a little wine for courtesy, especially with people who are accustomed to it, and who are offended by refusal.

103d. In Company of your Betters be not [longer in eating] than they are lay not your Arm but ar[ise with only a touch on the edge of the table.]

Chapter viii. 42. Quand les autres ont acheué de manger, despechez vous aussi, & ne tenez pas les bras sur la table, mais posez les mains seulement sur le bout.

When the rest have finished eating, you should do the same quickly; do not hold your arms on the table, but only place your hands on the edge of it.

104th. It belongs to y'e Chiefest in Company to unfold his Napkin and fall to Meat first, But he ought to begin in time & to Dispatch with Dexterity that y'e Slowest may have time allowed him

Chapter viii. 45. C'est à faire au plus honnorable de la compagnie de déplier le premier sa seruiette, & toucher aux viandes: & partant les autres doiuent attendre paisiblement sans mettre la main à chose aucune deuant lui.
46. Et au contraire il doit estre soigneux de commencer en son temps, de pouruoir à tout, d'entretenir les conuiez, & finir le tout auec telle addresse; qu'il donne temps aux plus tardifs de manger à leur aise, s'entretenant, s'il est de besoin, à gouster legerement des viandes, ou quand il est loisible de discourir à table; entremesler auec le manger quelque petit discours, afin que les autres puissent auec loisir d'acheuer.

It is for the most distinguished member of the company to unfold first his napkin and touch the food, and the rest should wait quietly, without laying hand on anything before he does. (46.) On the other hand, he ought in due time to commence, to consider everything, entertaining the guests, and managing all so adroitly as to give time to the more dilatory to eat at their leisure; if necessary for this, slowly tasting the viands, or, when table-talk is permissible, introducing a little chat during the meal, so that the others can finish at their ease.

105th. Be not Angry at Table whatever happens & if you have reason to be so, Shew it not put on a Chearfull Countenance especially if there be Strangers for good Humour makes one Dish of Meat a Feast[36]

Chapter viii. 47. Ne vous fâchez iamais en table, quoy qu'il aduienne, ou bien si vous vous fâchez, n'ent faites point de semblant, principalement y ayant des estrangers à table.

---

[36] Sidenote: Toner has 'but' instead of 'put' in this Rule.

Never be angry at table, no matter what may happen, or even if you have cause for anger, do not show it, especially if strangers are present.[37]

106th. Set not yourself at y'e upper [end] of y'e Table but if it be your Due or that y'e Master of y'e house will have it so, Contend not least you Should Trouble y'e company.[38]

Chapter viii. 48. Ne vous asséez point de vous mesme au haut-bout; miais s'il vous appartient, ou si le maistre du logis le veut ainsi, ne faites pas tant de resistance pour n'y point aller, que vous fachiez toute la compagnie.

Seat not yourself voluntarily at the top; but if the place properly belongs to you, or the master of the house so wills, do not offer so much resistance to its acceptance as to annoy the company.[39]

107th. If others talk at Table be attentive but talk not with Meat in your Mouth

Chapter viii. 49. Si on lit ou deuise en table, soyez attentif, & s'il faut parler, ne parlez point auec le morceau en la bouche.

If there be reading or chat at table, be attentive, and if you have to speak, do not speak with your mouth full.

108th. When you Speak of God or his Attributes, let it be Seriously & [with words of] Reverence. Honour & obey your Natural Parents altho they be Poor

Hawkins vii. 43. Let thy speeches be seriously reverent when thou speakest of God or his Attributes, for to jest or utter thy selfe lightly in matters divine, is an unhappy impiety, provoking heaven to justice, and urging all men to suspect thy beliefe.—vii. (*unnumbered*) Honour and obey thy natural parents although they be poor; for if thy earthly Parents cannot give thee riches and honour, yet thy heavenly Father hath promised thee length of days.

---

[37] Sidenote: Hawkins vii. 40. 'A cheerefull countenance makes one dish a Feast.'
[38] Sidenote: There is a blank in the MS. after upper.
[39] Sidenote: Walker: 'Desire not the highest place, nor be troublesome with impertinent debasing yourself by refusing,' etc.

*(There is nothing in the French Maxims corresponding to the
second sentence of Rule 108. The Maxim nearest to the first sentence is
the 9th of Chapter i.:—"Il se faut bien garder de prononcer aucuns
nouueaux mots, quand l'on parle de Dieu ou des Saincts, & d'en faire
de sots contes, soit tout bon, ou par raillerie." "Avoid irreverent words
in speaking of God, or of the Saints, and of telling foolish stories about
them, either in jest or earnest." Compare also the last sentence of
Maxim vii, 11, ante, under Rule 72.)*

109th. Let your Recreations be Manfull not Sinfull.

Hawkins vii. (*unnumbered*). Let thy recreations be manful not
sinful; there is a great vanity in the baiting of Beasts, the Bears and
Bulls lived quietly enough before the fall; it was our sin that set them
together by the ears, rejoyce not therefore to see them fight, for that
would be to glory in thy shame.

110th. Labour to keep alive in your Breast that Little Spark of
Celestial fire called Conscience.

Hawkins vii. (*unnumbered*). Labour to keep alive in thy breast, that
little sparke of Celestial fire called Conscience, for Conscience to an
evil man is a never dying worm, but unto a good man its a perpetual
feast.

THE END

Made in the USA
Middletown, DE
30 March 2024

52314689R00040